Pot for Profit

The Cultural Lives of Law
Edited by Austin Sarat

Pot for Profit

Cannabis Legalization, Racial Capitalism,

and the Expansion of the Carceral State

Joseph Mello

Stanford University Press

Stanford, California

Stanford University Press
Stanford, California

Printed in the United States of America on acid-free, archival-quality paper

Library of Congress Cataloging-in-Publication Data

Names: Mello, Joseph, author.
Title: Pot for profit : cannabis legalization, racial capitalism, and the
   expansion of the carceral state / Joseph Mello.
Other titles: Cultural lives of law.
Description: Stanford, California : Stanford University Press, 2024. |
   Series: The cultural lives of law | Includes bibliographical references
   and index.
Identifiers: LCCN 2023045881 (print) | LCCN 2023045882 (ebook) | ISBN
   9781503612280 (cloth) | ISBN 9781503639218 (paperback) | ISBN
   9781503639225 (ebook)
Subjects: LCSH: Marijuana—Law and legislation—United States. | Marijuana
   industry—Law and legislation—United States. | Drug
   legalization—United States. | Imprisonment—United States. | Race
   discrimination—Law and legislation—United States. | Racism—United
   States.
Classification: LCC KF3891.M2 M45 2024 (print) | LCC KF3891.M2 (ebook) |
   DDC 345.73/0277—dc23/eng/20231003
LC record available at https://lccn.loc.gov/2023045881
LC ebook record available at https://lccn.loc.gov/2023045882

Cover design and art: David Drummond / Salamander Hill Design Inc.
Cover photography source: Shutterstock

Contents

Preface

When I began writing this book what feels like a lifetime ago, in 2018, I thought it would be a quick project that I could wrap up in a year. People tried to warn me, "second books have a tendency to take longer than you think," but I didn't listen. Five years, a global pandemic, and a few major life changes later, this book is finally coming to fruition. It turns out second books really do take longer than you think. But second books are gratifying in so many ways, too. Writing without the pressures of the tenure clock and the watchful gaze of a dissertation committee has, for better or worse, allowed me to develop more of my own voice as an author. It has also given me the courage to explore new subject matters and try new research methods. All of this is, I hope, to the benefit of this publication.

Why weed? It's a question some have asked, others have probably wondered, but been too polite to ask. I have long found cannabis fascinating. I grew up in the Pacific Northwest, a region of the country that has always had a more permissive attitude toward the drug. As a child, it was not uncommon for me to spy a group or relatives discreetly sneaking away to smoke a joint at a family gathering. As an adolescent, I found it difficult to square the negative messages I received in school about the dangers of "marijuana" with the hard-working professionals and attentive parents I knew who smoked it. And, when a family member was incarcerated for a cannabis offense, I saw firsthand the destructive consequences of America's War on Drugs.

Many lawmakers have, however belatedly, come to understand these consequences as well. I have watched with some satisfaction as my home state of Oregon has adopted an increasingly progressive approach to cannabis over the years, becoming one of the first states to legalize cannabis for medical and adult use. As a political scientist I continue to be fascinated by changes like these. Today, our sclerotic political institutions seem hopelessly gridlocked and our courts outright hostile to change. Yet, in the past few decades the American public has undergone monumental cultural shifts in its attitudes toward once-divisive issues like gay marriage (the subject of my first book) and cannabis (the subject of this one). I wrote this book in part because I wanted to know more about how Americans navigate changes like these.

I write this book at a time of great economic changes as well. Technological innovations like smartphones, social media, and artificial intelligence are dramatically reshaping our lives, and the devastation of organized labor in the United States over the past five decades has made it difficult for workers to fight back. One effect of this is that corporations have come to exert increasing control over activities that had long been resistant to the pull of commodification and profit maximization. As an academic I feel this change acutely. Universities, ostensibly nonprofit institutions dedicated to academic achievement, have increasingly begun prioritizing things with more profit potential such as athletic programs, slick marketing campaigns, and large capital improvement projects—while simultaneously cutting back on the number of tenure-track faculty members. Similar dynamics shape everything from our experience at the doctor's office, to the way we shop for groceries, to the news we consume, to the way we order a ride or find lodging. At least initially, many believed that cannabis could offer an anecdote to the normal way of doing business in corporate America. I began writing this book in part because I wanted to see if they were right. Five years later, I no longer have much faith that cannabis can resist the power of corporate influence. However, I continue to be inspired by the work of many activists in this area, and I remain hopeful for the development of a more equitable cannabis industry.

This book would not have been possible without the help of many others. First and foremost, I'd like to thank the cannabis activists, industry workers, and cannabis business owners who spoke with me for this project. These complete strangers generously gave their time to an academic whom they had never met, who contacted them over email, pitching a vague idea for a scholarly book about cannabis. During our interviews many shared their personal stories in great detail, putting up with my annoying and, I'm sure, somewhat naïve questioning. This book quite literally would not have been possible without their insights.

I received financial support for this project from a variety of sources. The bulk of this research was funded by a fellowship from the Wicklander Institute for Business and Professional Ethics. Thank you to the Wicklander family for their generous donation, without which this research would not have been possible. Thanks also to the administrative team at the Wicklander Institute, especially Summer Brown, for her assistance in overseeing the distribution of the grant funds. Thanks also to the DePaul University Research Counsel, which provided both a summer research grant and a number of course releases that allowed me to work on this project. Finally, thanks to the College of Liberal Arts and Sciences at DePaul, which provided me with a Summer Research grant and a Late Stage Research grant to help support this project.

Thank you to the editorial team at Stanford University Press for helping to take this manuscript from an idea to a reality. My editor, Marcela Maxfield and her team, were extremely easy to work with and made the peer-review process one of the smoothest I have had so far in academic publishing. I also appreciate the work of my production editor Tim Roberts and my copy editor Therese Boyd, who helped to make the final version of this book as polished as possible. I am honored to have this book be a part of the prestigious SUP series on "the cultural lives of law," and grateful for the support of its series editor, Austin Sarat. Thanks also to the anonymous peer reviewers who evaluated this manuscript. Your feedback has greatly improved the quality of this work. I would also like to thank Michelle Lipinski, the previous editor at Stanford University Press, who first showed interest in this project and offered me an initial advance contract.

I received helpful feedback from a number of people during the writing of this book. I'd like to thank Jeff Dudas, Susan Burgess, David Williams, and Renee Cramer for providing helpful commentary on one or more versions of this project over the years. Thanks also to my colleagues in the Cannabis Studies program at DePaul, especially Don Opitz and Steve

Kelly, for helping me think through all things cannabis. I received helpful feedback and commentary on early versions of this research presented at academic conferences and symposiums from many people, including Will Garriott, Dominic Corva, Anna-Maria Marshall, and Jamie Huff, among others. I have enjoyed the continued support and mentorship of my colleagues in the Political Science Department at DePaul over the years, especially Scott Hibbard, Wayne Steger, David Williams, Val Johnson, Susan Burgess, Ben Epstein, Rose Spalding, and Christina Rivers. Also, thanks to our wonderful departmental support staff, especially Mihaela Stoica, Estela Sorenson, and our excellent contingent of student assistants.

None of this work would have been possible without the love and emotional support of my friends and family, especially my wife, Tessa Beukema, and my three children, Beth, Everett, and Landon. Tessa, I don't know how I would have done this without you. I mean that quite literally—carving out time to write, while working at a teaching-focused institution and managing our busy household would have been impossible without your help! Thank you for offering so many helpful insights, and for suggesting many of this book's best ideas. Thanks also for putting up with my constant blathering about cannabis these past few years, for listening to me as I test out the slightest variations in tone and sentence structure, and for helping to reassure me with positivity and enthusiasm when I grew frustrated with the writing process. Thank you as well to my kids for being such a wonderful distraction. Watching you grow up these past years is the most satisfying experience of my life, and it helps to keep everything else in perspective. Writing is a grind; there were many times when I felt beaten down by the process. Having my family around always helped pick me up. I love you all.

I feel so fortunate to have been given the opportunity to have the academic career that I have had. I entered the academic job market in 2012, at a time in which tenure-track jobs in political science were a dwindling commodity, but I was lucky enough to snag a coveted job offer from a liberal arts college in a desirable location. I am so thankful to everyone who helped me get through this process. I'll start with my mom, Jeannie, and dad, Frank Mello, who have been my biggest cheerleaders over the years. Mom and Dad, thank you for supporting me completely in everything that I have ever done, from youth soccer, to journalism, to wrestling, to debate, to academics. You are two of the hardest-working people I have ever met, I thank you both for teaching me to take pride in my work, to do things the right way, and to grind like none other. You always encouraged me to work hard and be the best that I can at whatever I do. That has served me well in life.

A number of teachers and professors have helped nurture my academic talents over the years. I continue to benefit greatly from the mentorship of some excellent scholars during graduate school, including David Yalof, Kristen Kelly, Virginia Hettinger, Steven Dyson, Michael Morrell, Jeff Ladewig, and Howard Reiter. Jeff Dudas, my dissertation advisor, mentor, and friend, has been a constant source of encouragement and support throughout my scholarly career. My undergraduate professors at Willamette University were the ones who most inspired me to become an academic in the first place. Willamette was a special place, and I would not be the writer that I am today were it not for the careful and considerate feedback of professors like Richard Ellis, Bill Duvall, Melissa Buis, Bill Smaldone, Samy Basu, and David Gutterman, among others. I'd also like to thank my various debate coaches and partners over the years, for helping me to refine my argumentation style and analysis. So much of how I think, write, and talk today has its roots in high school and collegiate debate. Thank you to Rachel Wilczewski for bribing me into joining the debate team at Sam Barlow High School with a chicken dinner from Boston Market. And thanks to Bob Trapp, Kyle Hunsicker, Muna Luqman, Rob Layne, Matt Lehman, Robert Veneman-Hughes, Paul Crisalli, and Andrew Swan for putting up with me as a college debater.

Finally, thanks to the many students who have influenced me over the years. Much of the material for this book first saw the light of day as part of a syllabus for one of my courses on the Politics of Drug Reform, Social Movements, or Introduction to Law and Society. So many of the ideas for this book were inspired by things my students said during class discussions, wrote in their papers, or mentioned during office hours. Thank you for allowing me to test out my ideas on you, for challenging me to see things from new perspectives, and for continuing to inspire me to teach and learn.

Pot for Profit

The Cultural Roots of Cannabis Reform

So much of the conversation [about legalizing cannabis] became dominated by typical economic incentives . . . that were divorced from justice in ways that were fairly disturbing. . . . I think that we didn't understand the ways that the economics of racial inequity in business at large in America was going to replicate itself in this area.
—Tamara (cannabis activist)

It's just been hurtful to watch how the Black community's been excluded, how the Black community has not been given true information on how to get into the industry, how to sustain in the industry. . . . Legal cannabis, man, is really a trick to me.
—Guy (cannabis activist)

We misarticulated what it was we were looking for. . . . We made a shorthand which said legalization. . . . We were actually asking for freedom in cannabis, but [legalization] . . . was merely the framework to allow those who misunderstand the plant to take control.
—Harriet (illicit cannabis business owner and activist)

Bob Marley and the Wailers had been performing professionally in Jamaica for nearly a decade when they finally broke through in the United States with *Burnin'* in 1973. The album caused a furor. Songs like "I Shot the Sheriff" and "Burnin' and Lootin'," which paint a dark picture of authoritarian terror, and compel listeners to rise up against the state using violent imagery, were terrifying to many white suburbanites. The album art was just as controversial as the music. The back of the album featured an artistic rendering of a defiant, dreadlocked Marley smoking a massive conical "joint" of cannabis, and the album included many full-color photos of Black men in Kingston sporting dreadlocks and smoking large joints. Marley biographer Timothy White explains how the American press initially reacted to the band:

> A lot of people believed that a Mau Mau–inspired cult of demonic antiwhite murderers had been uncovered in the Caribbean. The music conjured up images of white tourists being hacked to death on the fringes of tropical golf courses. . . . The American press . . . began running long, detailed pieces on this Jamaican cult that . . . smoked more pot than the populations of Haight-Asbury and Greenwich Village combined. It was a good story . . . falling right in line with the rest of the cult stories they'd been uncovering: the Manson family, the Lyman family, the Children of God, the acid churches, the suburban witch covens. (White 2006, 261)

This militant image of Marley persisted until after his death. Toward the end of his life Marley complained to his biographer that most reporters still treated him as "a novelty figure or a noble savage, surprise he could read, write or express himself beyond expounding on biblical tracts" (White 2006, 447).

The times they are a-changing. Today, Marley would probably be surprised to find that in many US states customers can now walk into a sleekly designed dispensary reminiscent of an Apple store and legally purchase a wide array of cannabis products branded in his name. "Marley Natural" is, according to the company's website, "the official Bob Marley cannabis brand" (Marley Natural 2022). The line is owned by the private equity firm "Privateer Holdings," a massive cannabis consortium based in Seattle, which also owns the popular cannabis brands "Leafly," "Docklight Holdings," "Left Coast Ventures," and the Canadian medical cannabis company "Tilray" (Seven Hounds Ventures 2020). It must compete for shelf space with other celebrity cannabis lines and their corporate sponsors, including "Willie's Reserve" by country singer Willie Nelson, "Chong's Choice" by comedian Tommy Chong, and "Leafs by Snoop" by hip hop artist Calvin Broadus Jr., better known as "Snoop Dogg" (Peake 2020).

These changes should be exciting for the cannabis activists, consumers, medical patients, industry workers, and business owners who make up what I will refer to in this book as the "cannabis community." Many have spent decades fighting for cannabis reform. They believe that the US government's highly punitive approach to drugs has been a destructive and ultimately futile effort—one that has caused untold damage to the lives of millions of Americans, especially communities of color (Criminal Justice Policy Foundation 2019; Drug Policy Alliance 2022; ACLU 2022). Some see the creation of a new legal cannabis industry, with its enormous profit potential, as a once-in-a-generation chance not just to end the destructive effects of cannabis prohibition, but also to repair some of the damage that has been caused by it (Koram 2022).

Yet, as the epigraphs at the beginning of this chapter indicate, legalization has not been the boon to these communities that many cannabis activists had hoped for. Though a few Black celebrities have been able to capitalize on the growth of corporate cannabis, most of the wealth produced by this new legal cannabis industry has become increasingly concentrated in the hands of those who already enjoy power and privilege. Only a tiny fraction of the legal cannabis businesses that are currently being operated in the United States are owned by people of color, and almost no one who suffered significant consequences from the War on Drugs is currently making money in the legal cannabis industry.

How did this happen? And what if anything can be done about it? In this book, I take up these and other questions by examining the project of cannabis reform from a law and society perspective. Cannabis has received an uptick in scholarly attention of late, with hundreds of interdisciplinary "cannabis studies" programs forming at colleges and universities across the United States (Avetisian and Stone 2022). This suggests that cannabis studies is an emerging field of academic research centering on the cannabis plant, the people who care about it, and the intellectual, social, and cultural contexts that give meanings to it (see, for example, Corva and Meisel 2022). Yet sociolegal scholars have, until this point, largely ignored cannabis (but see: Aviram 2015, 78–97; Garriott 2020). In this book I argue that law and society offers a unique perspective, with valuable insights to contribute to our understanding of cannabis reform. In the remaining sections of this chapter, I elucidate some of these contributions by providing a discussion of the scholarly debates that undergird the arguments made here. I then explain the research design and methodology used for this project and conclude with a brief overview of the arguments I make in subsequent chapters of this book.

A Sociolegal Perspective on Cannabis Reform

"Law and society" is an interdisciplinary approach to the study of law that seeks to move beyond the traditional court-centric focus of most legal scholarship. Sociolegal scholars challenge the conventional idea that legal meaning is the product of formal legal actors such as judges and lawyers. Instead, they conceptualize law as a bottom-up phenomenon in which sociocultural understandings filter into the courtroom, shaping the beliefs and actions of these actors. This insight can be seen as an extension of the realist critique of law that emerged in the United States during the early part of the twentieth century (Holmes 1897). Those scholars criticized the conventional understanding of law as an arena of reason in which questions are answered through dispassionate analysis of case precedent or legal statutes. They argued instead that law is a political process, and that legal decisions are often arbitrary or capricious.

One of the most fundamental insights of law and society scholarship is that law is essentially everywhere. The United States is a law-obsessed country. Whether we are aware of it, or not, our culture is shot through with legal symbols and discourse. This means that even though most Americans will spend little time inside of a courtroom, they will live their entire lives in the shadow of the law (Calavita 2016, 37–58). This creates an omnipresent legal culture that influences our thoughts and behavior in often imperceptible ways. These cultural understandings shape how we see the law and, in turn, these conceptions of legality shape the way that we see ourselves (Silbey 2005). In order to understand this dynamic, sociolegal scholars encourage researchers to focus on "the common place of the law" by studying how popular understandings of law are formed outside of the courtroom (Ewick and Silbey 1998; Gilliom 2001; Lovell 2012). These scholars often refer to the common understandings of the law that we develop as a result of this cultural contestation as our "legal consciousness" (McCann 1994; Engel and Munger 2003).

Perhaps no issue better demonstrates the cultural construction of legality than cannabis. Law is central to the project of cannabis reform. The word "law," in all of its various manifestations, is often used as a short-hand to indicate legitimacy by the people in this movement. The slogan most commonly used by supporters of cannabis reform is simply "legalize it!" and people in the cannabis community often talk about cannabis as a civil rights issue, or mention the need to "get legal," or "be legal." It is perhaps unsurprising that a community built around what has, until very recently, been an illicit substance would have a particular fascination with the law. Members of this community have grown accustomed to trading stories about drug busts, giving detailed information about existing drug laws, and providing legal advice to one another. These stories highlight a persistent fear of legal reprisal that has long permeated the cannabis community. Millions of cannabis users throughout the United States have lived under constant threat that they may lose their jobs, be incarcerated, or have a drug conviction placed on their permanent record. As a result, many in the cannabis community have chosen to keep their activities private, hiding out in what a number of my interviewees referred to as the "cannabis closet."

This is because cannabis prohibition has always been less about what cannabis does to us and more about what we think of the people who we believe to be using it. Drugs like cannabis are threatening to many because, they represent a loss of physical control, which clashes with Western notions of citizenship that place a premium on individual self-discipline (Manderson 1999, 182). This loss of control is particularly anxiety provoking when it is thought to be coming from racial, ethnic, or cultural "others." This is certainly the case with cannabis, which first became illegal in the United States as a result of moral panics directed at "deviant" racial out-groups, especially Mexican laborers and Black jazz musicians (Courtwright 2001, 39–46). During the 1930s newspapers often ran patently false, sensationalized stories of Black and Mexican "marijuana addicts" being driven insane, committing murderous crime sprees, and raping children (McWilliams 1990, 48–54). Later as cannabis became associated with the 1960s counterculture, cannabis users were derided as "burnouts" or "slackers" who rejected longstanding American values by expressing defiance toward authority and refusing to participate meaningfully in the economy (Himmelstein 1983; Baum 1996).

Making the Cultural Turn in Sociolegal Scholarship

In this book I make use of culturally informed scholarship in order to better understand the cultural contestation that is at the heart of the struggle for cannabis reform. Many sociolegal scholars have made the "cultural turn" of late, focusing on how law and culture intersect to create legal meanings (Calavita 2016, 171–88). "Culture" is a slippery term, and there are many different ways of conceptualizing it. One way that law and society scholars have sought to study culture is by articulating how cultural images are themselves a form of law. This approach, sometimes referred to as "law in the image" (Sarat 2000, 9), tends to focus on popular depictions of law that are found in books, movies, and television shows, in order to better understand how these images shape our legal consciousness.[1] Other sociolegal scholars have conceptualized culture by borrowing more heavily from legal realism. This scholarship examines the ways in which the cultural assumptions of a given society work to shape the construction of the formal "law on the books," as well as the more informal "law in action" (Mezey 2003). This suggests that legal meaning comes not from the top down, but from the bottom up, a concept that some scholars have termed "popular constitutionalism" (Schmidt 2018).

I engage with both notions of legal culture at times during this project. I am, however, primarily focused on understanding the cultural context in which cannabis legalization has emerged. I am particularly concerned with understanding how this cultural context has impacted the development of the cannabis reform movement, the construction of the legal regulations and policies governing cannabis, and the legal consciousness of the cannabis community. This cultural contestation is important because it shapes the parameters under which members of the cannabis community are able to successfully articulate new rights claims.

In the United States we often conceptualize rights as resources that are granted to all citizens equally. In the Declaration of Independence, Thomas Jefferson expressed a vision of individual rights that was universal, famously decreeing that "*all* men are created equal." But this "American creed" was, of course, written by a slave master, revealing itself to be more aspiration than reality. Indeed, one of the central insights of sociolegal scholarship is that rights are contingent resources (Dudas, Goldberg-Hiller, and McCann 2015). By this we mean that our willingness to recognize the legitimacy of someone's rights claim is dependent upon how closely the claimant emulates the characteristics of what is perceived to be a valued American citizen (Goldberg 2007; Bridges 2017).

This dynamic is no mystery to social movement activists, who have often sought to frame their cause in ways that will be more acceptable to a mainstream audience. Scholars of race and ethnicity have, for example, argued that members of minority groups frequently engage in "respectability politics" (see, for example, Higginbotham 1994, 185–230; Harris 2014). Marginalized groups often attempt to frame themselves as legitimate citizens who are deserving of rights, by distancing themselves from members of their community who fall outside the bounds of mainstream acceptability, while simultaneously elevating the visibility of those members who conform to widespread norms of cultural respectability.

Cannabis legalization has emerged as a viable policy idea in the United States during a time in which neoliberalism is culturally ascendent.[2] In this book I show how the cannabis community has coped with this cultural environment by engaging in a kind of "neoliberal respectability politics," elevating the voices of those in their community who conform to this ethos, while at the same time minimizing the visibility of those who do not. I show how some reformers have sought to challenge the stereotypical view of those who use cannabis as dangerous criminals or lazy slackers by offering a conception of the cannabis user as a "normal," productive citizen. Key to this shift in identity has been the cultivation of an image of those who use cannabis as industrious individuals who participate productively in the economy as workers, entrepreneurs, and consumers.

It is unclear what, if any, impact framing cannabis in this way *actually* had on convincing more Americans to approve of cannabis legalization. What is clear, though, is that many people within this community *believed* that framing cannabis in neoliberal terms would be beneficial to these efforts. As a result, they often wrote laws that constructed regulatory schemes for legalizing cannabis that favored corporate interests, and sidelined many longtime cannabis activists whom they perceived as hostile to this agenda. In addition to emphasizing the profit potential of cannabis, many advocates of legalization also sought to move cannabis away from its counterculture roots by minimizing the visibility of those within the cannabis community who do not fit well into this neoliberal narrative (Bender 2016; Schlussel 2017). Such a stance overwhelmingly benefits the primarily white, upper-, and middle-class Americans who have the business acumen and the financial means to invest in and profit from this new industry. However, it does little to help repair the damage done to Black and Latino communities, who have been the primary targets of punitive drug policies and who often face steep barriers to entry that prevent them from participating in the legal cannabis industry (Orenstein 2020).

Indeed, it is not entirely correct to say that some states have legalized cannabis for everyone over the age of twenty-one. It is more accurate to say that they have legalized cannabis for those privileged people who are willing and able to operate within the capitalist framework of the retail marketplace (Garriot 2020; Polson 2022). In this marketplace cannabis is often sold at prices much higher than is typically seen on the illicit or the unregulated market, and it is governed by a maze of formal regulations and informal customs, which require considerable legal expertise and legitimate business experience to navigate effectively. Instead of addressing these issues, many states have only added to these burdens by making it difficult for people with past cannabis offenses to expunge their criminal records and barring them from obtaining the retail licenses needed to operate a cannabis business legally. For many longstanding members of the cannabis community, it feels like legalization has left them behind.

Cannabis Legalization and the Carceral State

The US prison population has grown by more than 500 percent since 1980 (Sentencing Project 2023). This increased incarceration rate did not come about as a response to a rise in crime, but instead as a concerted effort to step up enforcement, particularly for low-level drug offenses (Garland 1990, 20; Gottschalk 2006, 23–26). Cannabis prohibition played a key role in creating this system of mass incarceration. Cannabis offenses accounted for 43 percent of all drug arrests in 2018, far more than for any other substance (ACLU 2020, 21). Though these arrests have declined of late, nearly 700,000 Americans are still arrested for cannabis offenses each year, more than the number of arrests for all violent crimes combined (ACLU 2020, 21). The brunt of this enforcement has been aimed at communities of color, especially Black people, who despite equal rates of cannabis use, are still nearly four times more likely to be arrested than whites for a cannabis offense (ACLU 2020, 29).[3] Indeed, the gap between Black and white arrest rates for cannabis offenses has persisted, even *increasing* in some states post-legalization.[4]

Nevertheless, there are signs that the American public is beginning to lose its appetite for mass incarceration. Several localities have recently elected "progressive prosecutors," determined to help dismantle the system from the inside (Davis 2019). Many of the activists and elected officials who helped legalize cannabis have been motivated, at least in part, by a desire to reduce the incarceration rate. Not surprisingly, legalizing cannabis typically does lower the number of cannabis arrests in that state, often quite dramatically.[5] But the government has a long history of co-opting well-intentioned criminal justice reforms, using them instead to perpetuate carceral power, and legitimate the continuation of past abuses (Gottschalk 2006, 238). As we shall see, legalizing cannabis does not necessarily mean reducing the state's ability to control those who buy, sell, or use the drug. Instead of giving up its power over cannabis, legalization has merely allowed government officials to exchange one mechanism of controlling this substance for another, more subtle, and much more effective one.

In his highly influential book *Discipline and Punish*, Michelle Foucault explains how power is wielded by modern nation-states. He traces the development of the state's ability to discipline its citizenry from the limited reach of the gallows, to the work gang, to the prison, to the omnipresent gaze of the modern surveillance state. At each step in its evolution the state adopts what are seemingly more humane ways of punishing, disciplining, or controlling those whom it perceives to be deviant. But these changes were not made for humanitarian reasons alone. They also allow the state to obtain new "machineries of power," which it uses to more effectively control its citizenry. In the final chapter of his book, "The Carceral," Foucault describes how state power becomes near total as it moves beyond the boundaries of the prison walls and spills into all areas of social life. For Foucault, all aspects of the modern state, including schools, hospitals, and workplaces, become part of the "carceral archipelago," sites of disciplinary power, where pupils are manipulated by a subtle system of "micro power" into becoming "docile bodies" (Foucault 1978, 297). These more subtle mechanisms of control work so effectively that the populace often does not even recognize that it is being controlled, making any efforts to challenge the power of the modern state much more difficult. In the final stages of this process, power is devolved to private corporations and other nonstate actors, making it even harder to identify and counteract (Gilliom and Monahan 2012).

The Racial Capitalism of Legal Cannabis

One of the most common ways in which people are controlled in the United States today is through our capitalist economic system. A growing body of criminologists, drawing on Marxist theory, have argued that the criminal justice system should primarily be understood as a mechanism used to control the poor and protect the capitalist economic order (Garland 1990, 83–130). Loïc Wacquant, for example, provocatively argues that "prison operates as a judicial garbage disposal into which the human refuse of the market society are thrown" (2009, xxii). Sometimes the state goes about this in obvious ways, by incarcerating poor people of color and placing them under formal control. Other times the state's influence is less obvious. When customers engage in routine financial transactions, for example, they may feel like they are doing so voluntarily, but the reality is that their actions are all backed by the coercive power of the state (Hale 1923). People do not passively follow the state's ever-changing rules governing cannabis because they think that it is the right thing to do—they do it because they know that if they do not do so, they may end up on the receiving end of state sanctioned violence (Cover 1986).

The shift toward policing cannabis through the "free" market poses a major problem for those who seek to use cannabis legalization as a mechanism for racial uplift. Capitalism has long been used as a tool for perpetuating white supremacy in the United States. As law professor Angela Harris tells us, "Racial subjugation is not a special application of capitalist processes, but rather central to how capitalism operates" (2021, vii). Racism is baked into our capitalist economic system, which relies on the existence of a permanent underclass of labor to be exploited. In the United States, as in much of the western world, that underclass has always been disproportionately comprised of racial and ethnic minorities (Jenkins and Leroy 2021).

There is perhaps no better historical example of the pernicious role of racial capitalism in America than in the failures of Reconstruction. In his exhaustive history *Black Reconstruction in America*, W. E. B. Du Bois lays the blame for the inability to build a more just and equitable society after the Civil War at the feet of America's capitalist economic system. He writes, "The slave went free; stood a brief moment in the sun; then moved back again toward slavery. . . . The resulting color caste founded and retained by capitalism was adopted, forwarded and approved by white labor, and resulted in the subordination of colored labor to white profits the world over" (1935, 30). In many ways, the economic potential of cannabis legalization mirrors the promises that the Freedman's Bureau presented to newly freed Black slaves more than a century ago. If we are not careful, we risk repeating the same mistakes.

Legal scholarship could benefit immensely from taking the ideas of racial capitalism more seriously. Though critical race theorists have long argued that law is a tool of white supremacy (Bell 1992), these insights have not always been applied to our economic system. Indeed, the subfield of law and economics is populated by scholarship that either ignores race completely or reduces it to an inefficiency that will surely be resolved by market forces alone (see, for example, Becker 1957; Epstein 1992). This has resulted in a legal system that is woefully unprepared to deal with the racial inequities at the heart of our capitalist economic order. Harris points out that:

> Antidiscrimination law, the primary place where race shows up in legal practice, provides individuals with tools with which to contest their exclusion from . . . institutions of the market and state—when exclusion can be proven to have been motivated by racial difference. But antidiscrimination law assumes that these institutions are otherwise race-blind and race free. Moreover, the remedies available under antidiscrimination law are designed to forestall collective economic redistribution as a possibility. (2021, ix)

This book remedies this oversight, by showing that our capitalist economic system functions not as a collection of neutral rules and regulations, where racism is an undesirable outcome, but as an inherently racist system that willfully perpetuates racial inequities.

The Long Struggle for Cannabis Reform

The fact that the retail cannabis market perpetuates status quo power structures in this way suggests that the work of cannabis reform activists will not stop with legalization. From their perspective cannabis legalization is merely one step in an ongoing multigenerational struggle for a more humane and socially responsible approach to cannabis. Yet the media, and even many members of the cannabis community, have often treated legalization as the ultimate victory for the cannabis reform movement. This tendency to focus myopically on major breakthroughs casts social movement victories as discrete events, disconnected from the larger historical context under which they emerged, and obscures the underlying power structures that they are attempting to combat (Dudas, Goldberg-Hiller, and McCann 2015, 371).

This flawed narrative is not unique to cannabis, it is a common lens through which social movements are viewed. Perhaps the best example of this is the American civil rights movement, a story that is conventionally told as beginning in 1954 with *Brown v. Board of Education*, and culminating in 1964 and 1965 with the passage of the Civil Rights and Voting Rights acts (Eagles 2000; Mattson 2002). This narrative strips the civil rights movement of its necessary context. Most troublingly, it ignores the backlash that these victories engendered, artificially constructing a progressive image of the United States as a country inexorably marching toward greater racial equality.

Such a telling is not necessarily wrong, but it is incomplete. As historian Jacquelyn Dowd Hall notes, "remembrance is always a form of forgetting" (2005, 1233). Remembering social movements in this way forgets a lot. It obscures the way entrenched power structures remain even after major victories, and makes the job of activists seeking to mobilize against these counter-movements even harder. It also lionizes the people responsible for these breakthroughs, ignoring the fact that their work builds on the efforts of generations of activists who came before them (McCann 2020). These ahistorical conceptions of social movement victories can be weaponized by opponents, who often point to major breakthroughs as evidence that the problems of the past have been solved, and construct efforts to build on these gains as illegitimate attempts to gain special rights or privileges (Crenshaw 1988; Hall 2005).

In this book I take these concerns seriously, conceptualizing cannabis reform as a multigenerational project that began long before cannabis legalization was a viable idea and will continue long after it has been achieved. I situate my discussion of successful campaigns for cannabis legalization in the middle of this book (chapter 2), flanked by chapters exploring the historical development of cannabis reform (chapter 1), and investigating how reform efforts persist after cannabis legalization (chapters 3 and 4). This more complete telling helps illuminate the ways in which legalization poses new challenges for social justice–oriented activists interested in cannabis reform.

Data and Methods

This work is theoretically and methodologically informed by interpretive social science. Scholarship that is oriented by an interpretive epistemology begins with the assumption that reality is socially constructed, and that the meaning we give to the world around us is necessarily mediated by cultural and linguistic understandings and normative assumptions (McCann 1996, 463; Hawkesworth 2006, 31; Yanow 2006, 75). Thus, the language that we use to talk about something like cannabis does not merely describe our reality; it actually constitutes it. Interpretive methods are ideally suited for exploring the cultural questions that are at the heart of the inquiry conducted in this book. I use an interpretive approach to help draw attention to how the ways in which we talk about cannabis shape who gets viewed as a responsible, rights-bearing member of the cannabis community, and who does not. These ideas help shape the formal legal policies that govern cannabis in the United States, as well as the informal ways in which these legal policies are enforced and implemented.

Interpretive social science operates under the assumption that the process by which people make meaning of their world is complex, dynamic, mutually constituted, and hotly contested (McCann 1996, 463). As such, interpretive scholarship rejects the positivist assumption that an objective researcher can isolate individual variables in order to make definitive causal statements (Hawkesworth 2006, 31; Yanow 2006, 75). Instead, interpretive scholars must explore how social, legal, institutional, and cultural norms work together to shape our understanding of the world

(Rabinow and Sullivan 1988, 14). As such, I am less interested in making definitive claims of causality in this book, and more concerned with drawing connections between the evolving culture of the cannabis community and the direction and development of cannabis reform.

The empirical core of this book is comprised of data that I collected during a series of forty-six in-depth interviews with cannabis activists and industry workers from 2019 to 2021. This research was carried out with the approval of my university's Institutional Review Board. To protect the privacy of my research subjects I have taken steps to preserve their anonymity by giving them pseudonyms and omitting identifying information. This gives my interviewees the ability to speak freely about controversial subjects without fear of harming existing relationships with other activists, elected officials, or industry stakeholders. It also protects them from legal liability, which is particularly important because many of these conversations involved the discussion of the use or sale of an illicit substance, in violation of federal and state laws.

I recruited my research subjects by soliciting pro-cannabis activist organizations such as the National Organization for the Reform of Marijuana Laws (NORML), Marijuana Policy Project (MPP), Drug Policy Alliance (DPA), and Americans for Safe Access (ASA). All forty-six of my interviewees self-identified as cannabis activists with the biggest groups coming from NORML (21) and ASA (10).[6] In addition to being activists, fifteen of my interviewees were working in the cannabis industry at the time of our interview (11 in the legal adult-use industry, and 4 in the illicit cannabis industry).

Effort was made to ensure a diverse sample.[7] Twenty-eight of my interviewees were men and eighteen women. Thirty-six of my interviewees identified as white and ten identified as nonwhite.[8] Regional diversity was taken into account as well, with interviewees from thirteen different US states included in the sample.[9] Most of my interviewees were based in states that had already legalized cannabis at the time of our interview, the largest numbers coming from Washington and California. Finally, as Erin Mayo-Adams correctly notes, most social-movement scholarship tends to focus on a small cadre of highly visible and well-resourced national activist organizations (2020, 5). In order to avoid this, I made an effort to recruit a mix of local grassroots-oriented volunteers and professional paid activists, working for national cannabis organizations. Thirty of the people I interviewed for this study identified as local activists, and sixteen worked for national cannabis organizations. Many of these local activists were affiliated with one of NORML's local chapters, which operate autonomously from the national organization.

These interviews were conducted using a semi-structured narrative or dialogic technique (Mishler 1986). This method encourages the interviewer to put the interviewee at ease by using an informal or spontaneous style and probing them with unscripted follow-up questions designed to get them to reflect critically on the role that they played in historic events. The goal of such an approach is to generate "a lengthy, dynamic, open-ended interactive dialogue in which interviewer and interviewee participate more equally in the common construction of meaning" (McCann 1994, 19). The purpose of these interviews was to better understand how these activists experienced cannabis legalization and how they understood its impact on members of the cannabis community. I was particularly concerned with how legalization has shaped the legal consciousness of these populations and how it has impacted continued efforts to mobilize for cannabis reform.

This interview data was supplemented with textual analysis of relevant source material. I utilized a variety of primary and secondary source documents for this project, including: campaign and advertising materials produced by cannabis activist organizations, stories about cannabis published in both mainstream and alternative media outlets, the biographies of notable cannabis reform activist, the works of counterculture authors like Norman Mailer and Hunter S. Thompson, and the music of rockstars such as Jimi Hendrix and Bob Marley. Whenever possible, I tried to use quotes directly from activists and other important figures themselves, typically sourcing them from biographies or other archival material, much of which is available online. I made substantial use of *High Times* magazine's online archives at times during this project, which contain more than 500 issues published from 1974 to 2018. *High Times* magazine is perhaps the best-known, and most widely read chronicler of the cannabis community, with more than 236,000 print subscribers and over 20 million unique online viewers a month (Murrieta 2017). The magazine is not without its critics (Schreckinger 2020), but examining it does provide a window into the evolving cultural identity of cannabis that cannot be found elsewhere.

Chapter Overview

This book consists of six chapters, including this introduction. Chapter 1 provides a historical overview of cannabis prohibition in the United States. This analysis proceeds chronologically with a focus on three important turning points that have shaped the project of cannabis reform—the passage of the Marihuana Tax Act of 1937, the launching of the War on Drugs, and the rise of the medical cannabis movement. I show how each of these events shaped the legal culture around cannabis, the goals and tactics of the cannabis reform movement, and the development of the US cannabis industry. My analysis here traces the evolving cultural understandings of cannabis in the United States and explores how changing ideas about who participates in this activity, and what values those populations espouse, have fueled cannabis prohibition. I also examine how this changing legal culture impacts the legal consciousness of those in the cannabis community, specifically, how participating in an illegal activity which the state has deemed "deviant" shapes how those in the cannabis community view themselves in relation to the law, and how these self-conceptions evolve as the legal treatment of cannabis changes.

In chapter 2 I shift my attention to the moment of cannabis legalization. I begin by examining how the changing culture of the cannabis community laid the groundwork for cannabis legalization. I show that early on cannabis use was synonymous with rebellion and an outlaw identity. Many activists who came from this community championed cannabis reform as a mechanism for progressive social change. The rise of a successful retail cannabis industry, however, brought more people into the cannabis space. Many of these people, particularly those coming from the business community, did not share these radical political beliefs. Indeed, many came to see the more radical elements of the cannabis community as counterproductive to their goals. As part of their efforts to build more popular support for cannabis reform, they engaged in what I term "neoliberal respectability politics," policing this community in order to hide those elements that did not conform to this ethos, while elevating the voices of those that did.

This influx of business interests into the cannabis community had an enormous impact on efforts to legalize cannabis. Corporate donors were able to use their considerable financial resources to shape cannabis legalization campaigns. They often wrote ballot-measure proposals that constructed regulatory schemes for legalizing cannabis that favored corporate interests and sidelined many longstanding cannabis activists, who they perceived as hostile to their agenda. This results in a regulatory structure for legal cannabis that primarily benefits those in the business community and fails to address many of the concerns of more social justice–oriented cannabis activists.

In chapter 3 I examine the regulatory framework that has grown up around the legal cannabis industry and explore its implications. On the surface, legalizing cannabis would seem to represent a reduction in state power. Yet a closer look at how the cannabis industry is regulated reveals that, instead of giving up its power over cannabis, the state has merely exchanged one mechanism of controlling this industry for another, more subtle, and much more effective one. I show how the state has used its power to regulate and tax cannabis to consolidate its control over the drug, bringing a marketplace that it has been unable to control through prohibition alone to heel through legalization. Legal cannabis states have used their newfound power to regulate and tax cannabis to create a legal cannabis industry that operates according to their terms. Those who wish to participate in the legal cannabis space must acquire all the proper licenses, pay the required fees, and comply with a maze of bureaucratic rules and regulations. These act as barriers to entry, preventing many people from being able to participate in the legal cannabis industry. As a result, the same predominantly Black and brown communities that were most adversely impacted by the War on Drugs are also the ones most likely to find themselves shut out of the legal cannabis industry.

Those lucky enough to obtain a cannabis business license must figure out how to navigate an extremely difficult business environment. Most cannabis business owners struggle to remain profitable and many fail. These difficulties are not felt by everyone equally. Those with prior business experience and more access to capital have an easier time weathering such a challenging business environment. Smaller, more independent operators, however, who often have less legitimate business experience and far fewer resources, struggle to survive. Minority-owned cannabis businesses are particularly vulnerable to these challenges.

Those who are unable to enter the legal cannabis space are forced to either leave the cannabis trade entirely, or continue operating in the illicit marketplace after legalization, even though doing so risks arrest. Though cannabis arrests have declined since legalization, they have not gone away. Thousands of people are still being arrested each year for cannabis offenses in legal cannabis states. This shows that legalizing cannabis should be understood less as a transition away from the policies of mass incarceration, and more as an attempt to redirect how police power is used, in order to better serve the state's interest in controlling the cannabis trade.

In chapter 4 I turn my attention to the state of the cannabis reform movement after legalization. This analysis helps illuminate some of the challenges facing activists who continue to fight for social change in the aftermath of a major victory. I document how cannabis activists working in legal cannabis states navigate the inevitable post-legalization decline, as they struggle to raise capital, build solidarity, and mobilize supporters without a highly salient cause like legalization to rally behind.

Cannabis legalization also changes the nature of the debate over cannabis from a relatively simple conflict between social justice–oriented cannabis activists on one side, and law enforcement officials and concerned parent groups on the other, into a complicated dispute involving a host of different actors. It creates new stakeholders, such as corporations, security companies, laboratory technicians, and commercial property owners, who have very different ideas about what cannabis reform should look like. It also has the effect of shifting the terrain of this debate from one-off political campaigns, which lend themselves well to grassroots organizing, to the constant grind of legislative rule-making, which does not. This further complicates the efforts of activists, requiring them to adjust their tactics and learn new strategies.

These challenges suggest that reforming the laws and regulations governing legal cannabis may be even harder than legalizing cannabis was in the first place. Shifting the debate over cannabis reform to a regulatory environment places activists at a disadvantage relative to deep-pocketed business interests, who use their considerable resources to hire lobbyists and influence the legislative process. This highlights the importance of drafting robust legalization bills, which put progressive values at the forefront, rather than accepting flawed cannabis legislation, in the hopes of reforming it later.

In the final chapter of this book, I provide an overview of the central insights of this research, then turn my attention to some lingering questions raised by this inquiry. Many of the longtime cannabis activists that I interviewed for this project have described legalization as akin to a "hostile takeover" of the cannabis community by the corporate sector. But a focus on the influence of corporate interests only tells part of the story. Here, I complicate this narrative somewhat by taking a deeper look at the values of the "original" cannabis community that many feel is being replaced—1960s counterculture. At least part of the reason that corporate cannabis has been so successful is that this community has never really been as progressive, or as hostile to corporate America as the stereotypical "hippie" image might lead us to believe. This is particularly true for race. Cannabis has always been framed in racially problematic ways, not just by the forces of prohibition, but also by the cannabis community itself.

Perhaps no one better demonstrated the difficulties of navigating race, capitalism, and cannabis in modern America than "Bob" Marley. Initially, the American media portrayed Marley in explicitly racist terms, often depicting him as an ignorant rustic, a stoned-out street tough, a sex-crazed maniac, or a militant revolutionary. This highly racialized image helped endear Marley to the American counterculture precisely because it allowed them to act out long-standing racial fantasies. As a result, Marley developed a dedicated following with the primarily white rock music audience in the United States, but he never really broke through with African American listeners. Following his death from cancer in 1981, a concerted effort was made to revitalize Marley's public image and broaden his appeal to a more mainstream audience. Beginning with the issuing of *Legend* in 1984, Marley was increasingly portrayed as a unifying figure of peace and racial harmony. This resulted in an extremely lucrative period of his career, with album sales far in excess of anything Marley was able to achieve while alive. But this sanitized portrayal was once again more concerned with servicing the evolving post-racial fantasies of Marley's still primarily white American fan base than authentically representing the anticolonial project of Black liberation that was so central to his music.

I offer Marley as a cautionary tale for those who seek to use cannabis to pursue progressive social change in the United States. Artists like Marley show the limits of working to advance political causes within the corporate space, particularly when those causes put you at odds with the economic interests of wealthy white people. Marley's experience suggests that Black people can succeed in this environment, but only by rendering their Blackness less visible, and only if they are willing to abandon the mission of racial egalitarianism for platitudes about diversity and racial harmony. This virtually guarantees that our efforts to improve racial equity in cannabis will never advance beyond the elevation of a few token representatives of the Black community, so long as it remains entrenched in the American capitalist system. In light of this history, the racially exploitative manner in which cannabis legalization has played out in the United States should not be viewed as aberrational. Instead, it should be seen as a continuation of the complicated racial dynamics that have always been central to the American counterculture and the mostly white New Left activists who identified with it.

ONE

Dispatches from the Cannabis Closet

Cannabis Prohibition, Legal Culture, and Legal Consciousness

We begin this inquiry with a historical overview of cannabis prohibition in the United States from the colonial era to the early 2000s. This analysis is designed to help readers who might not be as familiar with this subject matter develop a better understanding of (1) the changing legal and cultural status of cannabis in the United States, (2) the evolving "illicit," "medical," and eventually "legal" adult-use cannabis industry, and (3) the different strategies and tactics of the various individuals and organizations who advocated for cannabis reform during this time.[1] Understanding these historical dynamics is imperative for appreciating the broader implications of legalizing cannabis for adult use. It shows that legalization is an act of creative destruction, generating new rights and opportunities for some people, while at the same time taking opportunities away from others. It reminds us that the cannabis industry that is being constructed in states with adult-use legalization is not an entirely new entity, built on a blank slate. It is replacing an existing illicit industry and, in many cases, a lightly regulated quasi-legal medical cannabis marketplace as well. In this way cannabis legalization should be understood less as an instance of the state giving up control over this drug, and more as an instance of the state reducing its formal control, in exchange for more effective informal mechanisms of governing cannabis.

The Origins of Cannabis Prohibition

> The war on marijuana in this country is not about the plant, it's just an outgrowth of an ongoing culture war that continues to exist. It's not about marijuana, it's about what marijuana stereotypically represents to a certain group of people in this country.
> —Sean (cannabis activist)

The cannabis plant consists of three species, *cannabis sativa, cannabis indica*, and *cannabis ruderalis*, which have been used by humans for industrial, medicinal, recreational, and spiritual purposes for millennia. Archaeologists have found preserved cannabis buds used for religious rites in the gravesites of ancient Chinese Gushi people dating back to 2700 BCE (Lee 2012, 3–5). Some of the first recorded instances of what we might call "recreational" cannabis use come from the ancient Greek historian Herodotus, who took note of the Scythian steppe people "howling with joy" in their hemp vapor baths around 425 BCE (Crocq 2020). One of the first recorded medical uses of cannabis comes from the *Pen Ts'ao Ching*, a medical encyclopedia originally compiled more than 2,000 years ago, supposedly during the reign of mythical Chinese emperor Shen Nung. It lists cannabis tea as a remedy for more than 100 ailments (Pisanti and Bifulco 2019).

Cannabis in Colonial America

Cannabis as we know it in the United States today is a product of colonialism. The plant originated in Southeast Asia. It was brought to the African continent by Arab and Portuguese traders sometime during the first century, before being introduced to the Western hemisphere during the sixteenth century via the slave trade (Lee 2012, 15–19). European sailors quickly grasped cannabis's value. The plant could be woven into extremely durable yet inexpensive hemp fibers. Hemp is naturally resistant to salt-water corrosion, and thus makes excellent cordage for ropes, sails, and the riggings of ships. It is no exaggeration to say that the colonial project would have been made significantly more difficult without the wide availability of hemp fiber aiding the construction of a global trade network. As with other cash crops like tobacco and sugarcane, European traders quickly began establishing hemp plantations in the New World and even imported African slaves to work on them (Warf 2014).

Cannabis became such a valuable commodity that many early laws governing the substance actually encouraged its production. Indeed, the first official law concerning cannabis in the Americas was passed by Virginia in 1619, and it required every household in the colony to grow the plant (Schlosser 2003, 19). Many of the United States's founding fathers, including both George Washington and Thomas Jefferson, grew cannabis on their farms, even recording their experimentations with cannabis farming in their diaries (Lee 2012, 17–19). By the mid-nineteenth century, hemp had grown to become the number 3 cash crop in the United States, exceeded only by cotton and tobacco (19). Despite the prevalence of cannabis in the United States at this time, most Americans would have been unaware of the plant's psychotropic qualities. The cannabis plants that they were growing did not contained enough THC to cause intoxication.[2] The practice of smoking cannabis for medicinal or recreational use did not become widely known in the United States until the early twentieth century (Courtwright 2001, 43).

The cannabis that grew in warmer climates such as Africa and South America, however, contained more than enough THC to cause intoxication. The people who live in these regions have long known of cannabis's intoxicating effects. Since the plant grows like, well, a weed, it was usually cheap, easy to cultivate, and readily available to all. As a result, cannabis has often been primarily associated with poor and working-class people. Slaves, day laborers, and others accustomed to hard work used cannabis as a balm to sooth their sore muscles and ease the psychic pain of daily life. Overseers often encouraged workers and even slaves to grow the plant, observing that smoking cannabis was good for productivity (Warf 2014). The Mexican folk song "La Cucaracha" famously memorializes cannabis's ability to motivate displeased peasant workers. In the song the "cockroach," which represents a lowly foot soldier in Pancho Villa's rebel army, is unable to walk "Porque no tiene, porque no tiene/ Marijuana que fumar," or "because he has no, because he has no/ marijuana to smoke" (Lee 2012, 40).

Reefer Madness

Cannabis began to be seen less as an industrial product, or occasional folk medicine, and more as a dangerous substance in need of control, after it became associated with highly stigmatized racial out groups. The Mexican Revolution (1910–20) would ultimately compel more than 500,000 refugees to migrate to the American Southwest (Zong and Batalova 2014). Most historians credit these new Mexican laborers with introducing the practice of smoking cannabis to the American public (see, for example, Bonnie and Whitebread 1974), though more recent scholarship has questioned this hypothesis (Campos 2018).

Around this same time, cannabis would also become popular among jazz musicians, who celebrated the drug in songs like "That Funny Reefer Man" and "Sweet Marijuana Brown" (Jonnes 1996, 121–25). Unscrupulous newspaper publishers such as William Randolph Hearst sensed that the American public would be both enthralled and horrified by lurid tales of racial "others" engaged in hedonistic, drug-fueled escapades. They began feeding them a steady diet of sensationalized and often outright fabricated stories of Black and Mexican cannabis addicts being driven insane, committing murderous crime sprees, and raping children (Reinarman and Levine 1997, 5–8; McWilliams 1990, 48–54).

Government officials also worked to racialize cannabis in the minds of many Americans during this time. One way they did this was to stop using the more scientific sounding botanical name "cannabis," and begin calling the drug by its colloquial Mexican Spanish name "marijuana" instead.[3] This was done as part of a deliberate effort to get the American public to associate the drug with racial outgroups. Though the plant is still commonly referred to as marijuana by many in the United States today, many chafe at the use of this word, due to its racialized history (Coughlin-Bogue 2016). As one of my interviewees explained:

> Quit calling it *marijuana*. Cannabis is an old medicine. If you look in the

history books, you'll learn about cannabis. You'll know it was a very popular medicine in the United States. *Marijuana* came about all with the idea of prohibiting it. . . . To this day we keep calling it marijuana. And it's like that was only used to put on a negative. "Look at this new drug, marijuana, which is making people do crazy things. Black men are raping women and Hispanics are slaying families" and all this reefer madness.

Sensationalized stories of racial others committing heinous crimes while high on cannabis, combined with an explicit government policy designed to racialize the drug, helped to fuel public outcry. Soon, some government officials were calling for cannabis to be prohibited. The most vocal champion for the cause of cannabis prohibition in the United States at this time was Harry Anslinger. During his more than three decades as commissioner of the Federal Bureau of Narcotics, Anslinger worked tirelessly to rid the country of all drugs, including cannabis. Anslinger branded cannabis an "evil weed" and openly used explicitly racist appeals to demonize it. He is reported to have said that "there are 100,000 total marijuana smokers in the U.S., and most are Negroes, Hispanics, Filipinos, and entertainers. Their Satanic music, jazz and swing, results from marijuana use. This marijuana causes white women to seek sexual relations with Negroes, entertainers, and others" and that, "reefer makes darkies think they're as good as white men" (as quoted in Solomon 2020). The racialized hysteria that Anslinger helped create around cannabis culminated with the passage of the Marihuana Tax Act of 1937, which gave the federal government the power to enforce cannabis prohibition in the United States for the first time.

Cannabis and the Counterculture

Perhaps no period has had more lasting impact on our current cultural conception of cannabis than the 1960s. When people think about the "original" cannabis community, at least in the United States, they most likely picture the hippies, the Summer of Love, or Woodstock. Indeed, this period is so fundamental to understanding the current trajectory of cannabis reform, that I will return to it in the concluding chapter of this book. It was during this time that cannabis moved from being a highly stigmatized activity, associated primarily with the most marginalized elements of society, to the cultural mainstream. Unlike in previous decades, when cannabis was largely associated with groups that were already marginalized, the stereotypical hippies were young, mostly white, middle-class college students from more privileged backgrounds.

Many of these young hippies became involved in activism, but even so, they were less interested in accomplishing political goals, and more intoxicated with what historian Grace Hale calls the "romance of the outsider" (Hale 2011). Yet, these overwhelmingly white, relatively affluent, typically college-educated, young people had little occasion to experience being an outsider in their everyday lives. Smoking cannabis, which was both illegal and highly stigmatized at the time, allowed them to experience the titillation of violating not only the law, but also the established cultural norms of the day. As Michael Rossman, one of the leaders of the Berkeley Free Speech Movement, said, "When a young person took his first puff of psychoactive smoke, he also drew in the psychoactive culture as a whole, the entire matrix of law and association surrounding the drug, its induction and transaction. One inhaled a certain way of dressing, talking, acting, certain attitudes. One became a youth criminal against the State" (as quoted in Lee 2012, 95). For the young people who identified with the counterculture during this era, the fact that cannabis had long been associated with socially marginal individuals was part of its appeal. Using the drug was seen as an act of rebellion, a way to signal their rejection of the privileges given to them by birth, in order to make a political statement about the banality of this inheritance (Jonnes 1996, 205–99).

For young white Americans growing up during the 1950s and 1960s, no one embodied the romance of being an outsider more than people of color, especially Black people. During this time, white teens began embracing "Black" fashion, slang, habits, and of course Black music—especially jazz, blues, and later, rock and roll (Hale 2011, 49–131). Since cannabis was first introduced to the American public by Mexican laborers and Black jazz musicians, many saw their decision to smoke it in explicitly racial terms as well, some even going so far as to call themselves "white negros." No one embraced the white negro metaphor more thoroughly than counterculture journalist and author Norman Mailer. Despite being more than a decade older than the average hippie, Mailer, who cofounded the influential counterculture publication the *Village Voice* in 1955, was still a part of the counterculture milieu at the time. His infamous 1957 essay, "The White Negro: Superficial Reflections on the Hipster," chronicles the development of the budding countercultural scene in in New York city using language that is, at times, stunningly racist.

In Mailer's racial imaginings cannabis is the "wedding ring" that consecrates the marriage of Black and white, producing a kind of racial fusion that he later calls the "white negro." He writes:

> This particular part of a generation was attracted to what the Negro had to offer. In such places as Greenwich Village, a menage-a-trois was completed— bohemian and the juvenile delinquent came face-to-face with the Negro, and the hipster was a fact in American life. . . . Marijuana was the wedding ring. . . . And in the wedding of white and Black it was the Negro who brought the cultural dowry. (Mailer [1957] 2007)

It is not entirely clear what white people are bringing to this marriage (besides skin tone), but Mailer clearly believes that Black people are providing a "cultural dowry." This dowry largely consists of a mélange of crude racial stereotypes of Black people as primitive, hyperviolent, and hypersexual. He writes:

> The Negro could rarely afford the sophisticated inhibitions of civilization, and so he kept for his survival the art of the primitive, he lived in the enormous present, he subsisted for his Saturday night kicks. . . the pleasures of the body . . . and in his music he gave voice to . . . his rage and the infinite variations of joy, lust, languor, growl, cramp, pinch, scream and despair of his orgasm. (Mailer [1957] 2007)

Here Mailer plays on a common trope of people of color as primitive rustics, who due to their very primitiveness are able to more fully access a much simpler, more authentic, and somehow more morally pure, way of living (Murray 1989, 78–105; Hale 2011, 73–83; Hamilton 2016).

Mailer's crude, exoticized, racial musings are abhorrent to modern readers, but the tone of the essay is positive, even worshipful, of this imagined Black culture. Young white people who, like Mailer, developed a kind of cultural affinity for Black people based on these racist stereotypes, literally wanted to become Black. Yet, the fact that most of these new youth rebels were middle-class white kids, subtly shifted the portrayals of cannabis away from crude racist tropes to ones based on work ethic and a perceived lack of desire to conform to middle-class life. This ushered in a new era of moral hysteria around the drug. These new cannabis users were seen as undisciplined and deviant because they shunned established norms, expressed defiance toward authority, and refused to participate meaningfully in the economy (Himmelstein 1983; Baum 1996).

Many in the counterculture embraced this stigma and began engaging in what some have termed "cultural activism" (Rossinow 1998, 247). Groups like the "Diggers," the "Yippies," and the "Merry Pranksters" sought change, not through the political process, but through unconventional means such as establishing communes, using psychedelic drugs to promote "consciousness expansion," or engaging in performance art. The first formal cannabis activist organizations were born from these efforts. Beat poet Allan Ginsberg founded "LeMar," short for legalize marijuana, in 1964. It was the first organization dedicated to legalizing cannabis in the United States, but was poorly funded, and received very little attention—Ginsberg's rallies typically attracted a few dozen protestors at most (Lee 2012, 97–102). Another early cannabis reform organization, Amorphia, gained national attention after its cofounder, John Sinclair, was sentenced to ten years in prison for selling a small amount of cannabis to an undercover police officer. Amorphia organized a highly successful Freedom Rally, drawing public attention to the unusually harsh sentence, eventually leading to Sinclair's release. They were unable to turn this brief moment of intrigue into a sustained movement, however, and disbanded a few years later.

Developing a Domestic Cannabis Industry

Other cultural activists opted for a more direct challenge to America's cannabis laws. They began growing cannabis. Unlike cocaine or heroin, two drugs which must be imported to the United States, there is a long history of growing cannabis domestically in this country. As we have seen, Americans had been growing cannabis for use in industrial applications for centuries, but largescale domestic cultivation of cannabis for medical or recreational purposes did not begin until the 1970s (Johnson 2019). The most famous of these early cannabis growing communities emerged during this time in Northern California's Emerald Triangle.[4] This community of cannabis growers originated as an offshoot of the counterculture movement known as the "back to the landers" (Brady 2013). As youthful idealists they had been determined to challenge the consumerist culture of America and were convinced that they could foment a cultural revolution that would radically alter its values. But as the 1960s came to a dark and violent end, those radical dreams seemed far out of reach. Recognizing that they were powerless to change the culture of America, many of that generation sought instead to simply escape from it. The remote wilderness of California's redwood forests seemed like an ideal place to start over.

These early homesteaders came to this area with romanticized visions of living a simple life of rural poverty. Many began growing a few cannabis plants for their own consumption, or to help pay for basic necessities. But what started out as a few plants quickly grew into a very profitable industry. This was not something that anyone in this community could have anticipated. Since they were the product of a radical political culture that disdained the material lifestyle and capitalist ethos of America, the idea that they might get rich selling cannabis was unthinkable to them. It was also unthinkable because at this time most American consumers preferred cannabis grown in exotic foreign locals, referring to domestic cannabis derisively as "ditch weed." But the temperate climate of the Northern California coast is, it turns out, perfectly suited to growing cannabis. These natural factors combined with new cultivation techniques such as developing indica-sativa hybrids that could withstand cooler temperatures, the use of climate-controlled greenhouses with indoor grow lights, and the widespread process of producing seedless cannabis knowns as "Sinsemilla," would lead to the development of high-quality domestic cannabis.

This fledgling industry received another boost from an unlikely source during the late 1970s, when the United States government began aggressively policing the international cannabis trade. One of the most infamous of these efforts was the DEA's high-profile campaign to spray paraquat, an extremely toxic herbicide, on cannabis fields in Mexico. This highly publicized tactic made many cannabis consumers wary of foreign grown cannabis. Rumors of people dying from smoking cannabis tainted by paraquat proliferated (see, for example, Kornbluth 1978). These rumors turned out to be baseless, the toxic chemicals in paraquat are rendered harmless upon combustion, but even still, many consumers began to see domestically grown cannabis as a safer option (Johnson 2017, 120–22).

This success put the cannabis farmers of Northern California in an odd position. Carl, a cannabis reform activists who has collected oral histories from some of the original back to the landers, relayed to me the ambivalent attitudes that this success created, "it was a paradox that they had to deal with, which was that, they created a space basically, that normalized [the cannabis industry]. . . . These are folks that chose rural poverty and accidentally got a weird kind of life of rural prosperity." These dynamics sparked a generational divide amongst the cannabis community in this area. According to Carl:

> The old-timers [in the Emerald Triangle], they were, all of them, pretty upset about what they called, "greed growing," and folks who went big. . . . There's a difference between growing cannabis to sustain your livelihood and enrich your community and growing cannabis . . . only for money. . . . Corporate cannabis was out of whack [with their values]. . . . It was connected to . . . pesticide contamination and environmental damage. It was [also] the lack of connection to community, that the people who came in . . . weren't part-nered with the community, they were there to extract . . . money, and take it somewhere else.

In spite of this prosperity, many in the area held fast to their old counter-culture values. For them, opposition to the neoliberal consumer lifestyle was still fundamental to the culture of this community. They blamed out-siders for corrupting it.

Others, however, began to embrace growing cannabis as a potential means of gaining mainstream acceptance. A 1985 article in *High Times* magazine profiled some of the cannabis farmers in this community. In it the interviewer describes his subject as "a Presbyterian Kansas farmer's son . . . trained to derive the utmost return from the utmost effort, he'd probably be industrious at whatever he did" (Meyers 1985, 33). He then concludes that:

> The irony is that the Sinsemilla Farmer is in many ways the kind of self-made man that good American boys have always been encouraged to be. He's worked hard for his money, and the security of his family, he's built his own version of a new-aged energy-efficient dwelling, he's established a successful organic farming operation, and he's plowed a great deal of his money and energy back into the community he lives in. (Meyers 1985, 97)

The farmer's association with hard work and industriousness is a particu-larly powerful image for the cannabis community to evoke, as they have often been stereotyped as lazy and unproductive slackers. The farmer, on the other hand, has long been a heroic figure in American cultural mythology.[5] In this way, then, growing cannabis provided a middle ground for these individuals. It allowed them to rebel against what they saw as the established culture, yet still claim a sense of attachment to longstanding American values.

NORML and the Origins of the Cannabis Reform Movement

At the same time that the cannabis industry was beginning to gain a foothold in Northern California, a nascent cannabis reform movement was slowly developing as well. The cannabis reform movement did not really begin to get off the ground in the United States until the founding of the National Organization for the Reform of Marijuana Laws (NORML) in 1970. As one of my interviewees put it, "I don't know where you start [talking about cannabis reform] if you don't start with NORML." NORML was founded by Keith Stroup, a self-described Illinois farm boy, with financial assistance from Hugh Hefner. Heffner must have seen a kindred spirt in the cause of cannabis reform. After being lobbied by Stroup, he gave NORML its first $5,000 in seed money. He kept the organization afloat with additional donations during its early years and he gave NORML advertising space in *Playboy* magazine. This helped the organization gain much needed visibility, as no other outlet would agree to run their advertisements at the time (Stroup 2013).

NORML was formed in the wake of the passage of the Controlled Substances Act (CSA) of 1970, which classified cannabis as a Schedule I substance, and helped provide the legal basis for the highly punitive federal War on Drugs that would follow.[6] In its early years NORML focused primarily on providing legal aid to those who ran afoul of these drug laws and pushed for the decriminalization of cannabis. NORML activists had plenty to be optimistic about during the 1970s. The Nixon administration took a tough stance against cannabis, and the counterculture community that it was associated with. Nixon was embarrassed, however, when his "National Commission on Marijuana and Drug Abuse" issued a report in 1972 recommending that cannabis be decriminalized (Shafer et al. 1972). NORML seized on this report, using its findings to push aggressively for the decriminalization of cannabis at the state and federal level. Thanks to these efforts, eleven states passed laws decriminalizing the possession of small amounts of cannabis during the 1970s. NORML had its best opportunity for federal action on cannabis reform when Jimmy Carter was elected president in 1976. Carter, who had endorsed decriminalizing cannabis previously, began to soften laws against cannabis once in office. But he would ultimately back away from this position in the face of opposition from law enforcement.

As the name suggests, NORML was, by design, meant to be less radical than the cultural activists like the "back to the landers" who had come before it. The organization was interested in crafting an image of cannabis users as "normal," respectable citizens, and they adopted a strategy of pushing for incremental change through traditional legislative means. Sean, a longtime NORML activist, told me:

> Keith Stroup had formerly worked for Ralph Nader. And because Keith Stroup's formative years were spent . . . engaging in political advocacy . . . under the Ralph Nader model, he applied that model to NORML, and was very clear that NORML was a consumer advocacy organization. NORML's focus on policy and its mission statement falls back on what is best for the individual consumer.

Stroup's image of NORML as an organization focused on the cannabis consumer continues to shape the organization today. This has occasionally put them in conflict with more radical activists. As one activist I interviewed for this project told me:

> Consumer politics . . . they're super effective. That's the problem. Is that, they're like the only politics we get, when it comes to [cannabis] markets. . . . What's good for the consumer? Let's do that. That's one way in which NORML is a problematic organization to me, is that everything is about the consumer and getting the consumer to use the cheapest [product]. . . . The NORML paradigm really supports the Walmart-ization of cannabis.

It was not uncommon for me to hear criticisms of NORML during this research. Yet, even those who were critical still mostly agreed that, as the oldest and largest cannabis advocacy organization in the United States, NORML has had a positive impact on cannabis reform overall.

Today NORML remains a prominent player in the cannabis reform movement. Though its national organization is relatively small, it has a huge network of semi-autonomous local chapters spread out across the United States This gives NORML a large group of grassroots volunteers to draw from during what are typically state- or local-level campaigns for cannabis reform. Sean emphasized the importance of these local chapters to me during our interview, "NORML has always been a grassroots policy organization. We have a relatively small staff of paid employees. . . . But we do have a large number of volunteers in practically every state in America. Which lends itself to the sort of grassroots, state by state policy, which I think for marijuana just makes sense." Indeed, most of the local activists that I talked to for this study got started in cannabis advocacy through one of NORML's local chapters.

Cannabis and the War on Drugs

> In my experience as a police officer, the War on Drugs has been the most destructive, dysfunctional, and immoral policy since slavery and Jim Crow, and that's why I do what I do.
> —Michael (drug reform activist)

Any optimism that the cannabis community felt about the prospects for reform during the 1970s evaporated with the election of Ronald Reagan to the presidency in 1980. Reagan was elected on a law-and-order platform, promising a tough approach to crime and a renewed War on Drugs. This ushered in a dark period for the cannabis community. Congress passed the Comprehensive Crime Control Act in 1984, increasing federal penalties for possession of cannabis and establishing mandatory minimum sentences for drug offenses. Many states that had softened their drug laws during the 1970s, recriminalized cannabis during this period, imposing harsh punishments for its possession or sale. In addition to these punitive policies, the Reagan administration also made a concerted effort to discourage cannabis use by stigmatizing the drug. The most prominent of these efforts were First Lady Nancy Reagan's ubiquitous "Just Say No" campaign, the D.A.R.E. program, and Partnership for a Drug Free America, which launched a prominent advertising campaign warning about the dangers of drugs, including the oft lampooned "This is Your Brain on Drugs."[7]

Race and the War on Drugs

This more punitive approach to cannabis left deep scars on members of the cannabis community. Many of my interviewees recalled vividly the run-ins with law enforcement that they had during this period. Beulah, for example, told me how her experience of being arrested for possession of cannabis when she was in college changed her life:

> I got caught with over an ounce in a state with a zero-tolerance policy. So, I got charged originally with a felony. . . . They threw me in jail with horrible people. . . . This experience really kind of altered everything for me. . . . I lost my financial aid [and] . . . I just thought, oh, this is so wrong. . . . Now I have this charge that's going to follow me throughout my whole life and it can prevent me from getting a professional degree, and becoming a lawyer, and [keep] me out of college. I just didn't think that it was right.

Like most people who have run-ins with America's cannabis laws, Beulah was not required to serve significant jail time as a result of her arrest. Nevertheless, she suffered the loss of financial aid, lost the ability to go to law school, and suffered the embarrassment of having to inform her friends, family, and even her employer about these charges. Beyond that, the experience of being violently arrested by the police, put in handcuffs, and taken to jail was terrifying, leaving her with emotional scars that should not be easily dismissed.

Of course, part of the reason that Beulah may not have suffered even more serious consequences from her arrest is that, as a white person, she is protected by some amount of racial privilege. Sara, a Black cannabis activist, told me that when she was growing up in St. Louis, the police often overlooked the minor cannabis offenses of her white peers, but they treated her and her family more harshly:

> My little sister . . . her boyfriend . . . was actually a weed dealer, white kid, very wealthy. . . . [He] never really had to have an issue with police officers and he was dealing weed at my school! We had a resource officer and this cop had basically told him that "Hey, the police department knows that you're doing this. You should cut it out." The kid was afforded the opportunity to stop without having to go through the criminal justice system because of his privilege in St. Louis. My sister and him were caught smoking weed in the school parking lot. She got booked, she got taken away to the police station and he was let go.

As Sara describes, law enforcement officers have the discretion to determine for themselves whether one's cannabis use counts as a "youthful indiscretion" or a more serious offense. Race undoubtedly factors into this calculation. Studies show that implicit racial bias is widespread amongst police officers (Spencer, Charbonneau, and Glaser 2016).

Black men in particular are frequently harassed and treated with increased suspicion by law enforcement. Sara told me:

> My brother is a Black man in St. Louis. . . . [He] will get pulled over once a month at the very least. He got pulled over in our driveway one time! Cops always ask him if he's importing or exporting any illegal drugs every single time he gets pulled over. . . . Last winter, I was over in St. Louis to visit my family and my brother went out to get weed. . . . He was gone for a while. I had a bad feeling in my stomach. I could just feel it and he came home and he's like "Yeah, I got pulled over."

Getting pulled over by police is an anxiety-provoking situation under normal circumstances. The constant harassment from the authorities is more than just annoying, though. In a country in which unarmed Black men are routinely shot by police officers, it is potentially life-threatening.

The overpolicing of Black and brown men harms not just the individuals who are arrested, but their entire community. Guy, a Black man who grew up in a neighborhood where being harassed or arrested by the police for a cannabis offense was a frequent occurrence, told me that the War on Drugs was used to "destroy communities, destroy neighborhoods, destroy families, remove . . . an untold amount of wealth from the Black community, . . . and the men who were the business leaders of the communities." When asked to reflect on the toll that this experience took on him, he told me:

> The effects of the drug war are still being handed down through our community to this day. . . . I think I'm still dealing with the effects because nobody's ever offered us . . . any therapy for it. . . . They've never talked to us about home ownership, emotional intelligence, dealing with grief, nothing. . . . It's never been addressed anywhere. It was like it didn't happen in America, it's a piece of American history that nobody wants to talk about.

A word that Guy used repeatedly in talking about this experience during our interview was "trauma." I was struck by this, because our culture tends to fixate on the economic implications of racism, or the very real loss of rights that it may entail. We do not always mention its psychic damage, however, in part because it is less visible, and in part because men, particularly men who grow up in traumatized communities like Guy's, are often conditioned to avoid emotional vulnerability. Yet, it seems obvious that growing up in an environment where you experience near-constant harassment from the police and see many of your friends and family members arrested, or even killed, as a result of the War on Drugs, would be profoundly traumatizing.

The psychological scars of these repeated negative interactions with the law have a dramatic impact on the legal consciousness of these individuals. Many of my interviewees became so frustrated with the legal system that they began to see themselves as "up against the law" (Ewick and Silbey 1998). This has real implications for how and when these individuals choose to interact with the law more generally. For example, when I asked Guy if he had ever considered participating in the legal cannabis industry, he quickly dismissed the idea:

> When cannabis went legal. I never once ever, ever had the ambition of owning a license in the legal cannabis space, because . . . I knew what a lot of people don't understand—that [my state] . . . is one of the most racist states in the 50, but nobody ever wants to address it. And knowing that if I get a license . . . I'm going to be picked on by the inspectors and so on and so forth. And that's exactly what happened. They allowed maybe four Black people finally to get into the legal cannabis space, and those four Black people went through so much hell and trauma, they ended up losing their licenses. I think at this point there might be two Black people in [my state] with a legal cannabis license.

This suggests that ending the War on Drugs, and even legalizing cannabis, may not enough to repair the damage these policies have caused to the Black community.

This lack of trust in the government makes mobilizing people from these communities more difficult as well. The harsh treatment that people of color received during the War on Drugs has left many feeling a lack of efficacy, which discourages them from getting involved in politics. Sara, told me:

> I think that we, and when I say we, it's the Black community in general, are still healing. . . . It's one of those things where you've seen people being criminalized and vilified for so long, it's not something that you're going to be like,

"Oh, yeah, I will definitely jump into this thing." The only reason I feel like I'm comfortable doing [activism] is because I do come from a relative position of [economic] privilege as well. Somebody who is from Northeast St. Louis is not going to hop up and be like, "Oh yeah, I'm totally on board for this." . . . They feel disillusioned by politics because nobody has really been there for them. So why would they spend their time and their effort when somebody may be working two or three jobs, got two kids? . . . Why go through that extra effort when they're already sure no one is going to listen to a word they say anyway?

This very real difficulty in mobilizing activists of color, especially those from the communities most adversely impacted by the War on Drugs, poses a problem for the future of the cannabis reform movement in America. Historically, cannabis reform has been dominated by activists who are predominately white, cis gender, and mostly male. As a result, it has tended to advocate for policies that more closely represent the interests of those constituencies. Steering cannabis policy in a more progressive direction requires building a more diverse cannabis reform movement.

Outlaw Activism

Openly advocating for cannabis reform at this time took courage. Those who did so were fighting against a repressive state and swimming against the current of popular culture. Cannabis reform activists were forced to play defense during this time period, fighting an often-losing battle against the imposition of punitive drug policies. Those who spoke out faced intimidation; many served jail time as a result of their advocacy. Sidney, a longtime cannabis activist, explained it to me this way, "When my wife and I started this stuff in 1983, about 5 percent of the people thought we had some merit, and 90–95 percent of the people thought we were crazy. . . . We took risks. The things we did could put us in jail. A lot of my friends went to jail for speaking out about cannabis. Now it's no risk."

In addition to the physical risks that the cannabis community faced at this time, cannabis prohibition also had important psychic effects on those who chose to defy it. Law has powerful symbolic legitimacy in American politics. Americans respect the law in part because they know that the state has the authority to punish them violently if they fail to do so (Cover 1986), but also because they have internalized its moral legitimacy (Tyler 1990). This makes the very act of identifying as a member of the cannabis community during this time period an act of moral transgression. A number of my interviewees talked about how participating in an activity that the state deems morally wrong completely changed the way that they saw themselves, and the way that they saw the law.

For many, smoking cannabis caused them to question the legitimacy of the entire legal system. Jody told me, "I remember the first time I smoked weed and the first thought I had was, 'Oh my God, what else is the government lying to me about?' Because I'd grown up with . . . the Saturday morning cartoons and they'd have like, 'This is your brain, this is your brain on drugs. Any questions?' Like, I totally bought all that and then realized that they were lying to us." Guy had a similar reaction:

> Nancy Reagan [was] on TV talking about "Just say no to drugs . . . cannabis is bad, cannabis is this, cannabis is that," but yet . . . weed was part of my culture and my growing up, it was just around from day one. . . . I'm looking around at successful people with college degrees going to jobs every day, no addiction, their houses ain't dirty, they ain't dirty. It wasn't any of what the media portrayed these people to be in any way, shape, or form. From that moment, it was how can I trust this authority who's enforcing the law that is clearly against my people? And I understood this in like sixth–seventh grade, it didn't make any sense to me. And I lost all respect for authority very young because of it.

These experiences indicate that, at least for some people, prohibition may have had the opposite of its intended effect. Instead of building more respect for the law, it actually caused many who ran afoul of drug laws to grow more skeptical of all legal authority.

Clearly, many members of the cannabis community embraced their outlaw image and willingly violated US drug laws. Yet even the boldest of these individuals needed some way of justifying their activity, to reconcile the fact that what they were doing was illegal. For some, the language of rights provided a powerful mechanism for explaining why their decision to disobey what they believed to be unjust drug laws was justified. Jonathan, was particularly attuned to issues of social justice. He told me:

> My activism doesn't have to do with the drugs. It has to do with the actions

of the police and the violation of our civil rights. . . . Many years ago, I came to the conclusion that how long I lived was not as important as how I lived. Because life's all too short anyway. . . . One person can make a difference, and I've always had a strong feeling of I need to stand up. . . . This is an important struggle to me. It's a human rights struggle. It's a civil rights struggle, and I see a much bigger picture. And as Hannah Arendt said, "Those that stand by and do nothing are the guilty ones."

Scholars have long argued that such "rights talk" can be used by social movement activists to inspire people and mobilize them to fight for social change (Scheingold 1974; Zemans 1983; McCann 1994). Rights language is particularly well suited to this task, because rights have powerful symbolic legitimacy in American culture (Glendon 1993). Mobilizing this language allows cannabis users to see themselves not as criminals, but as full and equal citizens, entitled to the same rights and protections as everyone else (Engel and Munger 2003).

Others used moral logic to justify their decision to violate the law. Harriet, for example, explained that having the certainty that the cannabis she provides to medical patients saves lives helps give her the strength to continue engaging in civil disobedience, even though doing so risks arrest:

Yes, I do [welcome arrest]. . . . I do welcome it. I'm perfectly positioned for this. And I've got attorneys lined up and ready to go. Are you kidding me? . . . I've currently got about 25 kids that are doing a whole lot better than their peers in their cancer unit. You know? There's got to be something to this. I check with my moral barometer every morning when I wake up and decide whether I'm going to be a big old badass outlaw or not. And I shake my head yes, every day, because I'm not a bad person. My government paints me a bad person.

This is a particularly potent framework for those engaged in medical cannabis activism. Embracing medical cannabis imbued the cannabis reform movement with moral legitimacy. It would prove an effective means of challenging negative cultural constructions of the cannabis community, helping build more support for cannabis reform (Kilmer and MacCoun 2017).

But this outlaw framework is, in many ways, a privileged one. It is one thing for an older, middle-class, white person, who has a considerable amount of money, societal respect, and access to lawyers willing to assist them, to adopt an outlaw frame. It's quite another thing for a poor person of color, who has spent their entire life on the receiving end of legal violence, to do so. This is yet another reason that many of the most outspoken cannabis activists have tended to be white men. Sara told me:

> White people [are] always given the benefit of the doubt. But Black and brown people are not. . . . A white person who smokes but looks clean cut . . . they're a casual consumer. . . . A Black person who smokes weed is lazy, they don't have a job. . . . Black and brown people have to . . . live their lives being perceived as one way, trying to prove themselves different. Whereas white people have to show that they are . . . different than what we perceive them as. Good people. Hard-working people. On the straight and narrow. White people have to try really hard to fuck that up for themselves.

Indeed, people like Jerry Rubin, a white Yippie activists who was an outspoken proponent of cannabis, and a very visible member of 1960s counterculture, suffered no long-term consequences for doing so. In his later years, he became a very successful stockbroker!

The Cannabis Closet

Though many of the more radical activists that I interviewed for this study celebrated the outlaw status that came with expressing support for cannabis legalization at this time, others preferred to avoid legal reprobation by keeping their cannabis use secret. Cecil, a self-described "marijuana lawyer" and cannabis activist, explained it to me this way:

> Back in the day . . . the only people who were willing to come out of the closet as being marijuana consumers were the hippies and freaks. . . . I've always said that cannabis consumers were more in the closet than gay people, in that it's very easy to pass as a non-marijuana consumer if you're just careful about it. And it's been so attacked in our society that a lot of the consumers have been using it very quietly. And so, I think people have been very afraid to come out about that.

In addition to the legal risks, there is also a social cost associated with being a cannabis consumer that keeps many people "in the closet." Sean told me:

> If one was branded as a marijuana user, or even potentially having an interest in marijuana, not only was one potentially a criminal. . . . But in addition,

you were culturally stigmatized. So, for that reason, people who felt like they had something potentially to lose, a reputation, a career, a family, their children, even if they engaged in the use of marijuana, or were sympathetic to the idea of changing marijuana policy, that was generally information they were not going to share publicly. Because they felt, justifiably, that there would potentially be negative ramifications if they did so.

Members of the cannabis community could attempt to avoid the negative legal or social repercussions of these activities by keeping them secret. It is no surprise that many of them chose to do so. But living in the closet is not a comfortable existence. It requires submerging a core part of one's identity and limiting self-expression. Many in the cannabis community view cannabis as a highly effective medicine, or even just an enjoyable recreational activity. It is understandable that they would want to share this experience with others, and staying in the closet denies them the opportunity to do so.

Being in the closet also requires members of the cannabis community to live with the constant anxiety that they might potentially be exposed as a cannabis user. This fear is particular acute for parents, especially mothers. Judith captured these anxieties well when she told me:

> I'm a lifetime cannabis user. For 28 years I have used cannabis . . . but, being a parent and being a professional, I wouldn't go into smoke shops or "head shops," I would just purchase my [rolling] papers from the grocery store or convenience store. . . . I was in the closet because when you're a parent, unfortunately, there is that fear that okay, someone is going to try to take my children from me for using the cannabis plant. . . . That's a stigma that I really wanted to end.

Judith expresses a desire to end the stigma associated with cannabis use, but doing so is difficult when a sizable portion of your community is closeted. Particularly if those who are most likely to want to remain in the closet, are those who are most likely to be viewed as respectable by the general public.

A number of my interviewees shared with me how the cannabis closet complicated efforts to get people to commit to engaging in cannabis activism. Justin, for example, relayed to me how the cannabis closet frustrated his attempts to start a NORML chapter in his home state:

> NORML, one of their conditions to start the state-wide affiliate is that you

need to form a board, get five board members. Then adopt whatever by-laws and so on. So, I thought that would be easy as anything because I knew a lot of contacts. But I started going to them all and everybody was saying, "Geez, we'll give you financial help." "I can give you money." But they had a kid in school yet, and they really didn't want to be known to be on this board. Or, "the wife would kill me," even though they smoke pot . . . just, stay away from the cops and don't broadcast it, that's kind of the unwritten rule.

Even those who choose to engage in cannabis activism often work hard to keep their activities secret from at least some of the people in their lives. Nathan, a student activist, told me:

I try to hide my involvement in activism quite often. My parents are not really that supportive of the movement. They went from opposing to neutral now, I'd say, but they're still not very supportive, so that's not something they like to hear me talk about. Other than that, there's still a lot of stigma around the industry. I'm a president of the chapter [I work for], so it shows that I have leadership skills, but sometimes still I hide my involvement in my resume for jobs and stuff just because of that acceptance. Then the immigration thing just makes it harder. I'm worried that someone might find out about my involvement in this movement, and then try to use that as a way to try and deny my status. So that really does affect me and that's what makes me hide it sometimes.

Nathan, who was living in the United States on a student visa when I talked to him, was in the process of applying for a green card. His activism comes with enormous risks, and he is probably wise to mask it. Doing so comes at a cost, though. As a student with a relatively light resume, not being able to tell prospective employers about his skills mobilizing activists and leading protest campaigns limits his professional potential. Though staying in the closet may shield cannabis users from serious legal harm or social stigma, it still comes with significant sacrifices.

Overgrow the Government!

The stepped-up enforcement of cannabis prohibition during the War on Drugs had a big impact on the cannabis industry. The DEA, working in tandem with local law enforcement, engaged in a military-style campaign deigned to eradicate America's domestic cannabis industry. At least initially, these efforts were aimed primarily at the large outdoor cannabis farms of Northern California's Emerald Triangle. During the height of growing season agents used helicopters to spot cannabis farms from the air, and then swooped in to eradicate the plants and make arrests. Despite these harsh tactics, the US cannabis industry survived, in large part by moving underground.

Many cannabis producers decided that growing cannabis outdoors was too risky. In response they switched to more secretive indoor grow operations, which used sophisticated equipment and highly technical cultivation techniques. By the mid-1990s, most of the cannabis grown in the United States was being grown indoors (Johnson 2017, 136–39). The switch to indoor grow operations had a dramatic effect on the entire cannabis industry. Growing cannabis indoors allows an experienced cultivator to carefully control every aspect of the plant's environment. This results in larger yields, more potent cannabis, and increased profits. Growing cannabis in this way also has a much bigger impact on the environment. These grow operations use massive amounts of electricity. In order to avoid raising suspicion, growers had to create their own "off-grid" power supplies, often using crudely made diesel generators, which pollute the air and contaminate local waterways (Silvaggio 2018, 18).

Large, industrial-scale cannabis producers were not the only ones attracted to these new indoor cannabis growing techniques. Homegrown cannabis also saw a resurgence during this period. The pages of *High Times* magazine were filled with articles exploring the nuances of cannabis cultivation and encouraging readers to grow their own cannabis. A cottage industry developed to cater to these new consumers. Cannabis cultivation experts like Ed Rosenthal, and George Van Patten, who published articles under the name "Jorge Cervantes," became minor celebrities. Both men wrote reoccurring columns in *High Times* where they offered growing tips, answered questions from readers, and, of course, promoted their own line of cannabis cultivation videos and products.

Growing one's own cannabis was more than just a way to obtain cheap weed without ending up in jail. For many, it was also a deliberate act of civil disobedience designed to foment radical change. Many championed homegrown cannabis as a mechanism for challenging prohibition by encouraging Americans to "overgrow the government!" One of the best-known advocates of this approach was Marc Emery, a Canadian cannabis activist who is sometimes described as the "Johnny Appleseed" of the modern cannabis movement (Skye 2008, 72). His company, "Direct Marijuana Seeds," supplied cannabis seeds to growers across North America. He also founded the British Columbia Marijuana Party and ran for office on a pro-cannabis legalization platform multiple times. In a 2000 interview with *High Times* he summarized his outlook, "'Overgrow the Government!'—that's our campaign. We want people to grow lots of pot, to grow more pot than the government can destroy, to literally make it futile for government anti-cannabis programs" (as quoted in Skye 2008, 72).

Cannabis as Medicine

> Medical marijuana really changed the game. It allowed people to start publicly telling [their] stories. . . . All of the messaging in the world from the other side, saying things like, "Marijuana isn't indeed medicine," it is not going to offset the fact that these people know people, closely related to them, who have used marijuana as medicine.
> —Sean (cannabis activist)

People have been using cannabis, along with other herbs and plants, as folk medicine for centuries. Until very recently, there were few legal regulations governing the use of these botanicals. In the late nineteenth century Americans could legally purchase over-the-counter "patent medicines" and other elixirs that often included ingredients such as cannabis, cocaine, or opium. But the field of medicine was undergoing profound changes at this time. Medical schools were producing formally trained "professional" doctors who used new techniques and pharmaceuticals gleaned through the scientific method to practice "heroic medicine" (Starr 2017). These new medical experts were not only more professionalized, they were also almost exclusively white and male. In contrast, lay healers such as midwives, shamans, or faith healers were often women or people of color. They were seen as untrained and ignorant of modern medical science and their "knowledge" of these botanicals was disregarded as naïve and superstitious (Ehrenreich and English 2005, 37–110).

In the eyes of these medical experts, homeopathic remedies like cannabis were rough and dangerous medicines whose compounds could not be isolated, sterilized, and controlled the same way that synthetics could be. To them cannabis was "an effeminate interloper in the masculine world of real medicine, a dangerous drug pushed on a credulous public by illegitimate quacks" (Chapkis and Webb 2008, 13). It had to go. Cannabis was officially removed from the US Pharmacopeia and National Formulary in 1941, just four years after it had been effectively outlawed by the Marihuana Tax Act of 1937. When Congress passed the CSA in 1970, it classified cannabis as a Schedule I substance with "no currently accepted medical use." This legal classification not only barred doctors from prescribing it to their patients, it also effectively prevented medical researchers from studying it—complicating efforts to challenge this claim.

Mobilizing for Medical Cannabis

Despite these efforts, some people continued to use cannabis to treat various medical ailments. One such person was Robert Randall, a glaucoma patient who grew cannabis in his home for his own personal medical use. Randall was raided by the FBI in 1976, and his plants were confiscated. He sued the federal government, arguing that his cannabis use was medically necessary to prevent blindness, and citing the rarely used common law doctrine of necessity for support. The judge agreed and carved out an exemption to the CSA for medical cannabis patients (*U.S. v. Randall,* D.C. Super. Ct. 1976). This decision led to the development of the Compassionate Investigational New Drug Study program (INDS). Under this program the federal government sent cannabis grown at the University of Mississippi to a small group of medically approved patients, including Randall. This put the federal government in the awkward position of having legally defined cannabis as having "no medicinal value" in the CSA, while at the same time using government resources to maintain a compassionate use program for medical cannabis patients.

The notion that cannabis had no medicinal value would be further undermined during the HIV/AIDS epidemic. Hospitals were filling up with sick patients, and the few treatments options that doctors had available to them at the time caused extremely adverse side effects. Many of these patients began using cannabis to cope with their symptoms and found it to be immensely helpful. Phillip, a medical cannabis patient and activist, relayed his story to me:

> I tested positive for HIV back in '85. . . . And I started on . . . a drug program here that . . . tended to make people kind of sick. . . . You would have the heaves, you wouldn't be able to keep food down, you would become nauseous. . . . I had heard that cannabis would help with stomach issues. So, I tried it, and it helped me a lot. In fact, it helped me so much that . . . I was able to go to work and I was able to keep my food down and not become so nauseous. And so, I knew that there was something there that was really, really important for me, personally. And, I have been using cannabis ever since . . . and what I have learned from my doctor is that since I have been taking this [cannabis] tincture my CD4 cells have come to the point where they are normal, for somebody who wouldn't have HIV disease. And what that means is I'm going to be able to live . . . a complete life, and die of natural causes.

Cannabis was so effective at counteracting the symptoms associated with HIV that some activists began openly distributing it to sick and dying patients, in clear defiance of the law. Perhaps the most famous of these activists was Mary Jane Rathbun, affectionally dubbed "Brownie Mary" by her patients. She worked tirelessly as a volunteer in the AIDS clinic at San Francisco General Hospital in the 1980s, distributing cannabis-infused brownies to her patients during her daily rounds.[8]

The man considered by many to be most responsible for getting the cause of medical cannabis off the ground is Dennis Peron. Peron was a fixture in San Francisco's Castro District, where he fiercely championed the cause of medical cannabis and openly sold the drug to sick patients. His activities often attracted police attention. After a particularly brutal police raid, in which officers roughed up Peron's partner Jonathan West, who was in the final stages of his battle with AIDS, Peron vowed to fight back. He became the driving force behind Proposition P in 1991, a nonbinding local ballot measure that called for the state government to permit medical cannabis. The measure was treated as a joke by the media. Most experts predicted that it would be defeated easily. Not only did it pass, the measure carried 80 percent of the vote—a stunning victory. Peron opened his San Francisco Cannabis Buyers Club the very next year. It was the first public cannabis dispensary in the United States.

Peron's success gave a badly needed boost to the cannabis reform movement. Abel, a longtime cannabis activist, recalled his time working with Peron, and the importance of Proposition P:

> I think that the medical marijuana initiative was really key to everything. . . . I remember we were floundering around at that time. . . . But Dennis Peron . . . [said] hey medical marijuana might actually sell, at least in San Francisco, which was really liberal and at the time had the AIDS crisis going on. And a lot of AIDS patients were using marijuana for medicine. And the AIDS community was very well organized in San Francisco. And I thought that that was a very smart, strategic move.

Peron's triumph convinced many that pursuing medical cannabis through the ballot measure process could be successful. New organizations like the Marijuana Policy Project (MPP), which was founded in 1995, and the Drug Policy Alliance (DPA), founded in 2000, put renewed focus on running ballot measure campaigns and lobbying legislative officials to change cannabis laws. California (1996), Oregon (1998), Alaska (1998), Washington (1998), and Maine (1999) all passed ballot measures allowing cannabis for medical purposes during this time.

Pushing the Boundaries of Medical Cannabis Law

These early medical cannabis laws provided very little guidance or protection for those who sought to make use of them, however. Ballot measures express the will of the voter broadly, but the job of turning what is often just a one- or two-paragraph ballot measure into a fully fleshed-out law, is typically left to the legislature to complete after the election. In most of the states that passed medical cannabis ballot measures during the 1990s, the legislature simply refused to write laws providing more detailed guidance to medical cannabis users or providers. This forced them to operate in a legal gray area. As Harriet recalled, "All we had was an affirmative defense. . . . If we were arrested, we could go into court and say, 'Judge, the citizens of [my state] who rule supreme, have said that I can do this and I'm counting on you to follow the laws of our state. Which is citizens' rule.' That's all we had until 2008. So, it wasn't necessarily an easy place to be." Those who provided cannabis to medical patients risked prosecution from local officials who disregarded state law, and especially the federal government, who still enforced federal drug laws against cannabis, even in states that allowed it for medical use.

Jonathan felt this pressure acutely. He and his partner were targeted by the police after they began growing medical cannabis for AIDS patients during the 1990s. He told me:

> It really didn't hit home until the first bust in February 96, when our civil rights were just trampled on. . . . I just had to speak out and take on the cops, which led to very interesting results. . . . Over the years, we were served with six search warrants. Four of them were based on perjured testimony. After [one] bust . . . I did a demonstration about ending the drug war. Had post-cards printed, invited all the judges and prosecutors, and every lawyer to see how probable cause was conjured in [my] county. . . . The cops realized who we were, that we stood up to them. They wound up putting my partner . . . in the back of the police car [on an extremely hot day], windows rolled up, and he dehydrated. . . . I spoke out at Hempfest about what we had experienced. Ten days later, my lawyer got a letter from the DOJ saying that if we were ever busted again no matter how much the amount, that we would have federal charges done. . . . At that point, my lawyer took it to the *Seattle Times* and we were on the front page of the *Times*. . . . Then we got left alone for a few more years. . . . We were pretty radical.

Despite the tough tactics of the police, Jonathan and his partner were never convicted of a crime. Charges were dropped in each of these cases for a variety of reasons, including police misconduct or simple a lack of desire to prosecute. This was probably due at least in part to the fact that they drew so much sympathetic public attention, thanks to their public relations tactics.

Even when medical cannabis providers elude criminal conviction, though, "nuisance raids" conducted by law enforcement often have the effect of putting them out of business. Harriet explains, "The feds and everyone pile through the door. They seize all your cash. They seize all your inventory and they take you down and they arraign you or not. Close the shop up. You're out whatever cash you had on hand, whatever inventory you had on hand, and they're hoping you'll never reopen. This is how power fought back as the populous attempted to enforce their will."

Medical providers were not the only ones facing risks. Many medical cannabis patients were put in the difficult position of having to choose between using their medicine or obeying the law. Wanda, a longtime medical cannabis patient and activist, told me a powerful story about the difficult choices that she was forced to make during her pregnancy:

> I'm a medical cannabis patient, it's all up in my chart notes, and I'm pregnant. And what do I do? Do I switch to pharmaceuticals that I know are going to poison my baby? Do I keep using the marijuana when I know I could have my child taken away for that? Do I not use anything at all and hope I can survive the pregnancy and my child can survive the pregnancy? What is a person in my situation supposed to do?

After consulting with her doctor, Wanda decided to continue using the medical cannabis regime that was working for her, despite the potential legal risk it placed her in. She told me:

> I started to get really scared that if I continue to use this, I would have my child taken from me, and I started asking these questions about it . . . and by the time I got an answer from the social workers, I was twenty-two weeks pregnant and what they said was, "They always test any time they suspect cannabis; they test the cord blood and it shows you used all the way back to twenty weeks pregnancy." . . . Can you imagine what it's like to survive forty weeks, using cannabis, knowing it works for you and knowing every day you get closer to giving birth that you're closer to possibly losing your child? . . . It scared the shit out of me the fact of possibly losing my child to CPS.

Wanda's story about the fear she felt as a medical cannabis patient is exceedingly powerful, but her experience is by no means unique. Many of my female interviewees expressed similar concerns that the state might use their cannabis use as justification for policing their bodies or taking away their children.

Changing the Cultural Perception of Cannabis

Many cannabis reform advocates believed that focusing on the medical benefits of cannabis could be an effective way to challenge the stereotype of the cannabis user as dangerous other. In its place, they offered up a more sympathetic image of severely disabled, often terminally ill individuals, who simply want to use cannabis as medicine. One of the difficulties with this strategy, however, was that the medical community had long dismissed the idea that cannabis had medical value. Activists realized that if they wanted cannabis to be taken seriously by the public as medicine, they would need to change that. But this proved to be no easy task. Merely suggesting that cannabis might have medical value was controversial at this time. Even health care officials who believed that medical cannabis had merit were unwilling to say so publicly, for fear of harming their professional reputation. Ashley, a registered nurse and longtime medical cannabis activist, recalled:

> We tried to get clinicians to sign . . . a petition saying there's enough basic research to show the safety of cannabis and patients are reporting therapeutic value. "I support patient access to cannabis." Something of that nature. . . . And what we'd find out is healthcare professionals would say, "I'm with you, [Ashley], but I'm not going to put my name down." And that happened over and over and over again. . . . What we learned at that point was people are too afraid.

Doctors were not the only ones who were skeptical of medicinal cannabis; many potential patients had reservations as well. Harriet explained to me how patients who reach out to her with interest in using cannabis as medicine still struggle to cope with these internalized stereotypes, even today:

> [Cannabis] it's been demonized for so long. . . . I have mothers who call me. . . . First thing out of their mouth is, "my daughter is dying of a DIPG brain tumor. I've heard you might have something to help me, but I don't want my child to get high." . . . You're using the words of power to demean the product even as you're looking for a new way. . . . I tell all my patients, first thing, they say, "I don't want to get high." "Have you got an opiate patch on right now?" "Yeah." "Trust me, I can't touch that for high."

The idea that cannabis is dangerous or scary because it is intoxicating is something that a number of my interviewees reported continuing to be frustrated by. Ashley told me, "We even have elderly patients who come in and they say, 'well, give me that CBD, the nonintoxicating cannabinoid. . . . I want that CBD but don't give me the THC because I don't want to get high.' They're afraid that they've heard that if I get high, I'm going to lose control. . . . I won't know what I'm doing. It's like it's something bad." Henry, a retired school teacher and cannabis activist, dismissed the idea that just because cannabis can make you intoxicated, it must be bad or dangerous:

> A lot of people have a hard time accepting the duality of cannabis, that it's pleasurable and medical at the same time. And you know what I say? What

a wonderful new paradigm. That cannabis is so good for you and makes you feel good. Isn't that wonderful that a medicine that's good for you makes you feel good? Wouldn't it be nice if all prescription medications were not just good for you, but pleasant to take?

Gradually the American public has become convinced that cannabis had medical benefits (Felson, Adamcyzk, and Thomas 2019). This poses problems for federal officials determined to enforce cannabis prohibition. No matter what state law says, it is still the case today that buying or selling cannabis for any reason, even medical use, violates federal law and could put you in legal jeopardy (*Gonzales v. Raich* 2005). Yet, federal officials have found prosecuting cases involving medical cannabis providers to be more challenging than they may have expected. That is because cannabis activists have been able to use these arrests to focus public attention on the need for cannabis reform and generate favorable media coverage. Beulah told me:

> We had the DEA agents coming into California, and arresting patients and providers. So, we did a lot of work in the court system, helping people beat cases and try to make it so people have safe access. . . . If we knew someone was getting raided, we would show up there at the spot. We'd videotape it, we'd have protest signs, that kind of thing. . . . Also, a big thing that we do is we would go actually sit in the audience during their trial so when these medical marijuana providers or patients were in court trying to explain that they were doing this to help other people. When the jury looked out in the audience and saw it filled with people in wheelchairs and that looked ill, you know, they thought. . . . It'd really help people win some cases.

In this way, Beulah and others treated these courthouse confrontations as what social movement scholars have called "focusing events" (Kingdon 1995). Trials naturally draw a lot of media attention, making them ideal vehicles for activists looking to get their message out to a larger audience (Leachman 2014). This strategy was used to great effect in California, and other places, where the specter of law enforcement locking up people for providing medicine to patients who were clearly very ill sparked backlash, shifting public opinion in their favor (Hecht 2014, 106–20).

Developing a Medical Cannabis Industry

The legalization of cannabis for medical use had a dramatic impact on the development of the US cannabis industry. Early medical cannabis laws were ill defined. Medical cannabis ballot measures typically allowed "caregivers" to grow a certain number of cannabis plants in order to provide medicine to qualified patients. Beyond that, the industry was essentially self-regulated. This created a problem for many medical cannabis patients. The state told them that they could use cannabis as medicine, but gave them no information on how to access it. Some patients grew their own cannabis, others purchased it on the illicit market. But seriously ill people often do not have the ability to grow their own cannabis, and buying it on the illicit market defeats the whole purpose of legalizing medical cannabis in the first place.

Many patients found a solution to this problem by forming patient collectives. Wanda, who was a member of a cannabis collective in Washington, explained how these worked:

> The thing about the collectives was that people who couldn't grow for themselves, were too sick to grow for themselves, or whatever the case may be, could join together [with] others who knew how to grow. And then someone like me, who maybe doesn't know how to grow, and is too sick, but I have some money, I could pay the money for the electric bill so that all the other patients who don't have the money because they're disabled could get their medicine, too.

These collectives gave patients and providers a lot of freedom to structure their operation in ways which best suited their particular needs. Wanda told me, "Together we could pool our resources however we had to, to provide the product we needed to suit our group of collective patients. And that left a lot of freedom and wiggle room for meeting the needs of patients, whatever it took to do it. And there were a lot of people in that system who were giving it away for free . . . because it was more important to them to provide healing to people."

Though these collectives gave patients lots of freedom, it was unclear whether they were permitted under state law. Early medical cannabis states provided no information to people who wanted to set them up and performed little to no regulatory oversight once they were up and running. This lack of formalized structure left medical cannabis providers with little guidance as to how these collectives should be designed and, more importantly, what they needed to do to avoid legal reprobation. This was particularly problematic because, regardless of what state and local law said, the federal government remained committed to enforcing its federal prohibitions on cannabis. Indeed, many of these cannabis collectives were raided by the DEA during this time. Perhaps the most infamous of these raids was the one carried out against the Wo/Men's Alliance for Medical Marijuana (WAMM) in Santa Cruz, California, in 2002.

WAMM is, in many ways, a paragon for how medical cannabis can be provided with compassion, using a noncorporate model (Hecht 2014, 1–14; Chapkis and Webb 2008). Founded by Valarie and Mike Corral in 1993, it is one of the oldest nonprofit patient collectives in California. WAMM provided medical cannabis, as well as fellowship, and hospice care, to extremely sick and dying patients, often for free. The image of heavily armed DEA agents arresting wheelchair-bound patients was a public relations disaster for the federal government. The ensuing public outcry spurred the passage of S.B. 420 in 2003, which was designed to provide more protections for medical cannabis providers, in exchange for more regulatory oversight from the state. The raid on WAMM also sparked a drawn-out legal battle that ultimately culminated in a settlement with the federal government in 2009. As part of this settlement the Department of Justice issued the "Ogden Memo," named for its author, Deputy Attorney General David Ogden. This memo promised that federal officials would not prosecute medical providers who were in compliance with state and local regulations (Ogden 2009). This gave medical cannabis providers and patients a degree of legal protection that they had not enjoyed previously.

Both S.B. 420 and the Ogden memo were designed to protect patient collectives like WAMM. But the decision to trade more regulatory oversight from the state in exchange for increased legal protections would have the unintended effect of spurring the development of a new retail dispensary model of providing medical cannabis. Colorado is the state most responsible for initially developing this system. When Colorado legalized medical cannabis in 2000, it created a regulatory structure for its medical industry that differed sharply from the loosely controlled system of patient collectives that had existed in other states. In Colorado lawmakers created a tightly regulated industry that provided medical cannabis to approved patients via retail storefront dispensaries. The Colorado system, which was seen as safer, more controlled, and dramatically more profitable than the patient collectives had been, quickly became the model for regulating medical cannabis nationwide.

Retail storefront dispensaries have some benefits—they allow patients easier access, give medical providers the opportunity to earn a profit, and help shield them from federal prosecution to a degree not seen previously. But something was lost with the decline of the patient collectives as well. Many of these collectives had been designed to exist outside of the capitalist structure that governs most of the American economy. As such, many of the people who ran them were driven not by a desire to make profit but by a sincere belief that the cannabis plant was powerful medicine, to be given to patients at the lowest cost possible. Jennifer, who ran a medical cannabis collective in Washington prior to legalization, told me:

> In our state . . . a collective was supposed to share the expenses of growing the cannabis. So we did that, and . . . there were actually people that needed [cannabis] that didn't have money. Often, when you're sick, you don't have money, you've lost your job. And so, our goal was to try to get medicine to people at the lowest cost possible, pretty much. . . . I was giving medicine to people that needed it, that didn't have money to be able to buy their own. I was giving at least four people a gram a day of the full extract cannabis oil. Right now, in a store, it costs $40 to $60 for a gram of that, if you can find it.

If Jennifer were to give a sick patient cannabis for free today, she would be committing a crime in her state. Since insurance does not cover medical cannabis, legalization has forced many poor patients to go without medicine, or to go back to the illicit market, where cannabis prices are often cheaper.

In retrospect, the creation of retail storefront dispensaries was a turning point in the development of the legal cannabis industry. It shifted the identity of cannabis users from patients to consumers and, perhaps unintentionally, created the opportunity for a very profitable retail cannabis industry to emerge. As we shall see, the prospects of cashing in on this new industry brought many new people into the cannabis community—people who had no connection to the reform efforts that had come previously, and who had very different ideas about where to take cannabis reform next.

TWO

From Tie Dye to Suit and Tie

The Corporatization of Cannabis

Until very recently, legalizing cannabis was a fringe issue in American politics. No national politician was willing to express support for it, at least not publicly. Most denied ever even having used the drug.[1] This was probably smart politics. In 1969, when Gallup first began tracking the issue, only 12 percent of Americans said that they supported legalizing cannabis. Support for legalization remained tepid for the next half century, bouncing from a low of 16 percent in 1989, to a high of 32 percent in 2008 (Brenan 2020). In the last ten years, however, cannabis has gone mainstream. In 2018 67 percent of Americans said that they supported legalizing cannabis for adult use, and a staggering 91 percent supported allowing cannabis for medical use (Felson, Adamcyzk, and Thomas 2019). Expressing support for legal cannabis is so noncontroversial these days that even conservative political figures like former Republican Speaker of the House John Boehner have become outspoken proponents of it.[2]

This newfound public acceptance of cannabis has generated profound changes to America's drug laws. As of this writing, cannabis, a drug for which the US government has been sending people to prison for nearly a century, has been made legal for adult use in twenty-four states and the

District of Columbia.[3] More than half of all Americans currently live in a state where cannabis has been legalized. Though cannabis is still federally prohibited as of this writing, proposals to change those laws are being seriously considered by Congress for the first time.[4] What was once a deviant activity, only to be engaged in openly by the most marginalized, has begun to be seen as a legitimate, and potentially lucrative, business venture. More than $13.2 billion was spent on legal cannabis in the United States in 2019. It is estimated that sales will top $35 billion by 2025 (New Frontier Data 2020).

These changes would seem like positive developments for the cause of cannabis reform. But this "green rush" has also had the effect of bringing new corporate stakeholders into the cannabis community, creating tensions with existing members. Some longstanding members of this community have embraced the business sector. They believe that a more business friendly approach has helped improve the American public's perception of cannabis, and they welcome the substantial financial contributions that these corporate entities have made to the cause of cannabis reform. Others, however, have felt sidelined by these newly ascendant corporate interlopers. They believe that the cannabis reform movement has engaged in a process that I term "neoliberal respectability politics," elevating the business community's profit-obsessed vision of cannabis at the expense of the more social justice–oriented outlook that had been central to the project of cannabis reform previously. Though most support legalizing cannabis in principle, they lament that it has come at the expense of the core values and people, that this community has advocated for historically.

Cannabis Goes Corporate

> You believe corporations runnin' marijuana? (How that happen? Ooh)
> —Killer Mike and El-P (Run the Jewels, "JU$T")

Tensions between the more profit-minded and more social justice–oriented elements of the cannabis community are nothing new. Though cannabis has long been associated with the counterculture, complaints about excessive profiteering within the cannabis community go back to at least the 1970s (see, for example, Thompson 1970). Even so, cannabis legalization has greatly accelerated the commodification of cannabis. One way to see how corporate influence has changed the culture of the cannabis community is to look at how cannabis-themed publications have shifted their coverage of cannabis over time. Countercultural publications such as *High Times* magazine were instrumental to the development of the early cannabis community. During the 1970s cannabis was an underground activity, too controversial for serious discussion in mainstream media outlets. Outsider publications were some of the only places where an unapologetically pro-cannabis viewpoint could be expressed publicly. In a pre-internet world, spaces like these were essential to helping likeminded people find each other and begin to build community. As such, they are a great place to see the evolving cultural identity of this early cannabis community.

From Outlaws to Consumers

Founded in in 1974 by Tom Forçade, a former drug smuggler and radical Yippie activist, *High Times* magazine is the oldest and most popular chronicler of cannabis culture in the United States. Early issues of *High Times* magazine reflected the outsider ethos of its founder. They were filled with stories with headlines like "Pot, Peasants, and Pancho Villa" (Lemmo 1975), "Interview with a Smuggling Ace" (Morrison 1976), and "Drug Store Cowboys" (Butler 1977). These articles told romanticized tales of outlaw drug smuggling operations, and gonzo stories of drug fueled escapades. The magazine was more than just a how-to guide for drug smugglers though. This outlaw spirit was undergirded by a radical political message. In a 1976 interview, Forçade, using the alias "Leslie Morrison," expounded on the politics of drug smuggling, stating that, "To a great extent smuggling is a form of social protest . . . the people who get into smuggling are for the most part social misfits; they're nonconformists, they're antisocial people. . . . They're not compliant with society's rules. They're opposed to society" (Morrison 1976, 30).

These stories tell us something about the culture of the cannabis community during this time period. They all share a common celebration of individuals who live on the margins of society and offer overt challenges to the law. Though these figures embody some of the qualities that Americans have always found desirable in good citizens, these stories acknowledge that most would not fit comfortably in polite society.[5] This outsider perspective was central to the identity of the early cannabis community, especially the American counterculture. Since cannabis was illegal, associating with it necessarily meant calling into question the legitimacy of America's drug laws.

This questioning did not stay confined to cannabis prohibition, but often led to skepticism of the entire American legal system, and the underlying power structures that benefit from it as well. Kenneth, a cannabis activist and business owner, told me how using cannabis helped radicalize him:

> To be a queer person means that I am constantly . . . wondering what is on the other side of what society says is the way that things should be. . . . I think as a closeted teenager, who was walking around with what I now understand was a tremendous amount of anxiety about being who I was. While I didn't really understand that cannabis was doing this at that time, what it was showing me was that I can drop my shoulders, I can be who I am, even just for those few hours of being stoned, and then I would come out of that space and be like, "Well, holy shit. There is another way to be." I think that I always want to pull my experience of queerness across the intersections of identity and saying. . . . "How do you smoke weed and then stay indifferent?" How is it even possible to not smoke a joint and be like, "What's on the other side of this whole racism conversation?" …Cannabis is kind of this healing tool that helps people to begin to sketch through their fear and their guilt and their privilege.

Indeed, members of the cannabis community have frequently formed alliances with other social justice causes such as: gay rights, racial equity, gender equity, and organized labor, to name a few (Reiman 2022).

In recent decades however, *High Times* has become less focused on fomenting radical opposition to US drug laws, and more focused on working within the system to take advantage of the economic potential of cannabis. The magazine now regularly features articles with titles like, "Seed Fortunes" (Skye 2011), "The Booming Business of Buds" (Bernstein 2014), and "Turning Green into Gold" (Johnson 2015). These stories depict the cannabis industry as a green rush with enormous profit potential. This emphasis on the cannabis industry is accompanied by a concerted effort to commodify and commercialize cannabis. Nearly half of every issue of

High Times was dedicated exclusively to advertising in 2018, up from an average of 20 percent during the 1970s.[6]

This increased corporate focus has altered the relationship between the cannabis community and the law. In earlier decades, taking part in the cannabis community had always been framed as an act of rebellion. But lately, the community has become less concerned with challenging the law and more focused on using legal compliance as a way to gain mainstream acceptance. Though cannabis is still illegal at the federal level, many in the industry believe that if they grow or sell cannabis openly, in accordance with local and state law, then federal officials will view them as responsible, legitimate business owners, and leave them alone. As one grower remarked, "I'm not hurting anybody. . . . I pay my taxes; I drive the speed limit" (as quoted in Skye 2011, 56). This is a common strategy for socially marginalized groups, who often "speak the language of the law" as a means of building trust and showing worthiness (Williams 1991, 147).

These changing attitudes call into question many of the values that the cannabis community was founded on. Instead of creating a cannabis industry that reflected the radical political ethos of the early cannabis community, legalizing cannabis seems to have caused the cannabis community to adopt a more profit-minded corporate ethos. This has been a huge disappointment to many of the activists who pushed so hard for legalization in the first place. Jody, a cannabis activist and business owner, told me:

> The original cannabis community are really amazing people, right? They be-
> lieve in love, they believe in equality, they believe in a little bit of rebellion.
> They're pretty funky. I really like those people, and I think making a differ-
> ence is important. And I still believe that the cannabis industry could be the
> first socially conscious industry. . . . However, now being in the legal industry
> . . . we're competing with billionaires. . . . All they want is money, money,
> money. And that is pushing back on really the soul of the plant and where we
> all come from and what it could do.

Neoliberal Respectability Politics

Some longstanding members of the cannabis community lament the corporatization of cannabis culture. Others, however, see these changes as beneficial. They believe that a more business friendly approach to cannabis will help make the drug more acceptable to politicians and the American public. Creating a more business friendly image of cannabis requires more than simply talking up its tax benefits, though. It also requires finding people who can credibly carry this economic message and elevating their visibility within the movement. Cecil is a longtime cannabis activist and self-described "marijuana lawyer." He emphasized the importance of having more "responsible" members of the cannabis community be the face of the movement:

> I was lobbying Congresswoman Debbie Dingell a couple of years ago . . . and she was telling us that she really thought that marijuana was not good. That it made people basically stupid and lazy, and I became really upset, and just kind of outed myself. And I interrupted her, and said, "Do you know, Congresswoman, I've been smoking marijuana since I was 15 years old, and I have four college degrees and I'm an Eagle Scout. And I'm on the state Bar of Michigan representative assembly, and I'm a leader in my field, and pretty well respected among the Bar. And the reason why you have that impression, that people are losers and whatever, is because you're only seeing a skewed cross section of the society of people who are consumers. . . . The people who are calm, reasonable, responsible consumers stay out of the newspapers, and you don't hear about them, and you don't know about them." . . . I think I moved Debbie from hell no to no that day, [but] . . . after legalization passed, Debbie Dingell showed up on the steps, and was the first. . . sitting Congress person to speak at Hash Bash. . . . So, she's come a long way, and part of it is, I think, my outing myself.

Cecil's experience aligns with what some social scientists have called the "contact hypothesis" (Allport 1954). This theory holds that the best way to change the minds of those who harbor prejudicial views against marginalized communities is to facilitate more interpersonal communication between these groups. Doing so, it is hoped, will cause both parties to reconsider longstanding prejudices, and find commonalities.

The contact hypothesis only works, however, if the marginalized people who "come out" to the general public as cannabis users offer a perspective that cuts against existing stereotypes. As such, this approach does not just ask the more "respectable" elements of the cannabis community to speak up, it also asks, at least implicitly, that certain "undesirable" elements of the cannabis community make themselves less visible. One way we see this dynamic play out in the cannabis community is on the question of physical appearances. Many of my interviewees emphasized the importance of looking professional when advocating for cannabis reform in order to fight against existing stereotypes. For example, Jody told me:

> When I walk into a meeting . . . I don't have dreadlocks; I don't wear tie-dye. I put on my pearls; I look like the system. And I like a three-day music festival as much as the next guy, but when we're trying to change a bureaucratic system, we have to look and talk like them. . . . I remember walking in one day to a bill at legislative committee, and it was basically . . . all these business, nice-looking people that were trying to annihilate medical [cannabis], and then there were all these poor, not very nicely dressed, larger people that were saying, "Hey, this is my medicine. I need this. You're going to destroy what I have. This is a horrible idea." And they just got run over. They shouldn't have even shown up because the government did not care. They don't comprehend people that don't look like them and act like them.

Ashley expressed similar concern about the unprofessional attire of many cannabis reform activists. "NORML, when they'd go to doing things . . . it's like 'please dress up.' You know? 'Look professional, don't come in tie-dye.' It's what everybody's stereotype of us, 'just a stoner, they don't do anything but sit on the couch.' Cheech and Chong kind of image." Cecil agreed, "If we're going to a township to try to convince them to pass an ordinance, we don't need a bunch of hippies with long beards and tie-dye, and needing showers, coming in and going, 'Yeah, we want to come here and buy weed.' But if we can get a group of professional . . . people to dress up in suits and ties and sit in the front row, that's a whole different reception."

To many the idea that you should dress formally when talking to an elected official may seem like nothing more than basic professional advice. Cecil told me, "I wear tie-dye, but I wear suits [too], and there are different get-ups for different occasions. . . . Dress for success, that's the way politics is, that first impression makes a difference and appearances matter, and yeah, 'you can't judge a book by its cover,' but not everybody acts that way." Many community organizers have given similar advice to activists. In his 1971 book *Rules for Radicals* Saul Alinsky implored would-be activists to communicate "within the experiences of [their] audience," by framing their cause in ways that are relatable to the people that they are trying to convince, and by avoiding psychological barriers to communication, such as unconventional fashion styles. He even went so far as to tell young male counterculture activists during the 1960s that they would be more effective messengers if they would please cut their hair (Alinsky 1971, xix).

Obviously, there is an element of elitism at work here. Imposing strict standards of professionalism on people, such as requiring them to wear suits for formal occasions, reinforces problematic class hierarchies. Not everyone can afford to buy a suit or dress professionally; that should not make their perspective any less valid. These standards have been particularly problematic for groups that have been marginalized historically. Many feminist theorists and critical race scholars argue that professional dress codes have been weaponized against women and people of color, who are often accused of dressing in a manner that is too provocative or too ostentatious, in order to justify excluding them from areas traditionally dominated by white, cis-gender, men (Anderson 2015; Rios 2015; Rees 2018).

Corporate Influence on Cannabis Legalization Campaigns

> I welcome corporate cannabis. [We] struggled for decades with no money. . . . It is only with the backing of corporations who are pursuing cannabis for their own selfish purposes, to make money, that they're willing to spend the money to overcome the misinformation that the government's been putting out for decades. So, I think that, although I don't agree with all the corporations on all of their issues . . . the overall impact of corporate involvement in cannabis has been very positive for marijuana reform.
> —Charles (cannabis activist)

Corporate America's embrace of cannabis has had an impact, not just on the culture of the cannabis community, but also on the fight to legalize cannabis in the United States. In previous decades cannabis legalization campaigns were typically scrappy grassroots efforts led by enthusiastic, but often inexperienced, volunteers. Though they raised an admirable amount of money from small donors, and typically earned at least 44 percent of the vote, none of these early efforts was successful (see table 1). As cannabis became more socially acceptable, however, corporations began to take a more active role in these campaigns. As a result, more recent attempts to legalize cannabis have typically been run by professional campaign operatives, with significant financial resources at their disposal. They have also been more successful. voters in Colorado and Washington who approved ballot measures to legalize cannabis in 2012, making them the first states to do so. Seven more states would agree to legalize cannabis for adult use from 2012 to 2018 (see table 1).

This created a dilemma for the cannabis reform movement. Some longtime cannabis reform activists welcomed the resources that corporate donors could provide. Others chaffed at the outsized influence that these new donors, most of whom had no prior connection to cannabis, had on the direction of their campaigns. It is unclear what, if any, impact support from the business sector *actually* had on convincing voters to approve cannabis legalization. What is clear, though, is that many people within this community *believed* that corporate support would be beneficial to these campaigns. As a result, they often wrote laws that constructed regulatory schemes for legalizing cannabis that favored corporate interests, and sidelined many longtime cannabis activists whom they perceived as hostile to this agenda.

A Hostile Takeover of Cannabis Campaigns

One of the most obvious ways in which corporations impacted these legalization campaigns was through their financial contributions. With few exceptions campaigns in support of cannabis legalization have been able to outspend their opponents by significant margins (see table 1). This is thanks in large part to the work of two national cannabis advocacy organizations, the Marijuana Policy Project (MPP) and the Drug Policy Alliance (DPA). From 2004 to 2016 MPP contributed almost $17 million to cannabis legalization ballot-measure campaigns, and DPA contributed more than $8 million. Another $10.5 million was contributed by the New Approach PAC, a political action committee dedicated to a variety of pro-

Table 1. Cannabis Adult-use Legalization Ballot Measures, 2004–2018

				Money Spent	
State	Year	Title	Outcome	For	Against
Alaska	2004	Measure 2	Fails 56-44	$1,243,185	$34,807
Nevada	2006	Question 7	Fails 56-44	$4,403,878	$324,958
California	2010	Proposition 19	Fails 54-46	$4,647,242	$396,177
Colorado	2012	Amendment 64	Passes 55-45	$3,531,287	$738,774
Washington	2012	Initiative 502	Passes 56-44	$6,450,488	$16,718
Oregon	2012	Measure 80	Fails 53-47	$564,787	$74,375
Alaska	2014	Measure 2	Passes 53-47	$1,131,057	$191,516
Oregon	2014	Measure 91	Passes 56-44	$10,215,432	$328,165
Ohio	2015	Issue 3	Fails 64-36	$21,521,905	$2,203,718
Arizona	2016	Proposition 205	Fails 51-49	$6,582,376	$8,674,638
Nevada	2016	Question 2	Passes 55-45	$3,698,114	$3,771,081
California	2016	Proposition 64	Passes 57-43	$29,338,769	$1,675,670
Maine	2016	Question 1	Passes 50-49	$3,466,439	$278,713
Massachusetts	2016	Question 4	Passes 54-46	$6,875,418	$3,079,026
North Dakota	2018	Measure 3	Fails 60-40	$77,005	$254,082
Michigan	2018	Proposal 1	Passes 56-44	$1,728,653	$2,435,232

Source: Compiled by author using publicly available data from Ballotpedia (Ballotpedia.org) and the Institute for Money in State Politics (followTheMoney.org)

gressive causes, including legalizing cannabis for adult use (see table 2). These organizations all bundle donations from private individuals and corporations, causing many local activists to complain that they are too responsive to the interests of their wealthy donors. Several wealthy individuals also gave millions to support cannabis legalization campaigns directly during this period. Some of the biggest such donors include Silicon Valley billionaire Sean Parker ($8.5 million), prominent trial lawyer John Morgan ($6.8 million), philanthropist George Soros ($6.7 million), and hedge-fund manager Peter Lewis ($6.1 million) (see table 2).

This influx of money shifted the focus of these campaigns, alienating many in the cannabis community. In California, for example, many local activists were upset when Parker, who made his fortune as the founder of Napster and president of Facebook, spent $8.5 million to sponsor a can-

Table 2. Largest Pro Cannabis Adult-use Legalization Donors, 2004–2016

Donor	Total
Ohio License Group	$21,218,586
Marijuana Policy Project	$16,846,589
New Approach PAC	$10,599,872
Sean Parker	$8,960,245
Drug Policy Alliance	$8,372,506
John Morgan	$6,834,692
George Soros	$6,740,000
Peter Lewis	$6,189,329
Fund for Policy Reform	$6,140,000
Bob Wilson	$2,800,000
Barbara A. Stiefel	$1,750,000
Henry Van Ameringen	$1,525,000
SK Seymour LLC	$1,444,098
OR House Democratic Campaign Cmte	$1,241,385
Jacob Goldfield	$1,100,000
Dr. Bronners Magic Soaps	$1,015,000
John G. Sperling	$1,000,000
Nicholas J. Pritzker	$900,000
Ghost Management Group	$860,000
Thomas Cody Swift	$767,138

Source: Orenstein and Glantz 2020.

nabis legalization campaign in 2016 (Robinson 2016). They recalled with
bitterness how Parker was able to use his financial resources to squeeze out
longtime cannabis activists, and push for a more business-friendly adult-
use legalization bill. Henry, for example, told me:

> Two years prior to [the initiative being on the ballot] there was an organiza-
> tion statewide called the Coalition for Cannabis Policy Reform. CCPR. And
> we wrote an initiative called CRTA. "Control Regulation Tax Act." That was
> a much more progressive legalization initiative. And we were promised by the

Drug Policy Alliance and Marijuana Policy Project and . . . Weedmaps two million dollars . . . to put it on the ballot and run a reasonable campaign. At the last minute, they yanked all the money and decided to go with Sean Parker's attorneys, who wrote an initiative called [Adult Use of Marijuana Act] AUMA, and they had had no experience writing a cannabis initiative and they didn't consult with anyone from the community. . . . We were screwed by that. . . . It was a terrible initiative, it wasn't vetted with our community, we were stuck with it.[7]

In addition to shaping the details of the bill, Parker's team also edged out a lot of the volunteer activists who had been fighting for cannabis reform in the state for decades, in favor of what they considered to be a more professional organization. Beulah told me, "We tried to offer ourselves up to the actual campaign, but they really didn't want any help from the [activists] . . . I don't think they thought the campaign [that failed to pass in 2010] was . . . professional enough to really appeal to the whole state's audience. So, this time around they hired a high-priced firm to control all of that."

The business-friendly perception of Proposition 64 caused a rift within the cannabis community. Many activists made the painful decision to oppose the bill, despite the fact that they personally supported legalization. Brenda, a longtime cannabis activist and cannabis business owner in California, told me:

I opposed 64 and I actually had people hate me for it. . . . But I was able to just say matter of factly, "it's not the right bill." Just don't jump on this because it's the first one. . . . The people complaining about the taxes, I'll ask them, "did you vote yes on 64?" and if they answer yes, I said, "well it's your own fault. If you would read all 96 pages you would have seen that this is coming." . . . I think Prop 64 was the wrong bill to present and I think . . . the people [who] are doing well with it are the big corporations that [had] the money to back it. And I saw that coming.

Brenda's concerns were echoed by activists in other states as well. Washington's legalization initiative, for example, was criticized by many in the cannabis community for being too friendly to corporate interests, and not doing enough to protect medical cannabis patients. Perhaps the most controversial aspect of the bill was that it did not include any provisions allowing home-grown cannabis. One activist told me, "I had a big problem with [Washington's] bill. . . . It didn't allow the regular people to grow their own. It creates a hard situation where it's forcing those who . . . are too poor to be able to afford buying legal cannabis . . . the inability to have their own medicine and grow their own medicine at a cheaper rate. And to me that's an inequity and isn't fair application of the law." Indeed, in many states the price of legal cannabis is much higher than it was on the illicit or medical market. This forces many medical cannabis patients, who had legal access to cannabis prior to legalization, to go back to buying cannabis on the illicit market, even though doing so risks arrest.

Not everyone was so pessimistic about the prospects of continuing to use cannabis reform to address social justice concerns, however. Many expressed frustration with the way that these cannabis legalization bills were written, but believed that these errors could be fixed later. Henry, for example, spoke passionately to me about the myriad problems he had with Proposition 64, but when I asked him if he thought that passing the bill was a mistake, he quickly dismissed the idea. "I think it's good that we legalized it. . . . I don't think it was a mistake. I'm saying it was flawed. We passed the first civil rights laws. They were not perfect. We passed the first Social Security Act in 1935. It was not perfect. It has to be improved and evolve." Similarly, Tamara, who has worked in some capacity on nearly all of the cannabis legalization ballot-measure campaigns that have taken place in the United States since 2012, told me, "Every bill that has passed so far is a flawed bill in some way or another, right? Every single one of them. . . . [Being] wary about what it is that we're accepting in a flawed bill is more important than asking for perfection because . . . we're never going to get perfection. It's public policy." Compromise is essential to passing legislation in the American political system, where power is diffuse and change tends to occur incrementally.

But reforming legalization bills after they have been passed has proven to be harder than many of these activists could have imagined. Tamara herself admits to being surprised by this:

> I believed wholeheartedly . . . "we have to accept these excessive regulations . . . in order to appease the worried parents of the community, and that'll be okay, and we'll turn it back once people calm down a bit." But what is happening is that the trash-locking company and the security camera company gains . . . power in the state legislature with the regulators, and once they have a lock on that market, they're not going to give it up. So, you end up with these immovable pieces of an absurd regulation that are not based on

need, or common sense, or community input. . . . So, I think that you end up
with more entrenchments than most of us were able to anticipate at the time,
because we were justice advocates not business advocates.

Such concerns are particularly acute for people of color, who have a long
history of being disappointed by government promises of reform. Sara
told me:

> I think that the old guard feels like . . . let's legalize and get it done. No, it is
> about how [we legalize cannabis]. . . . We can't afford to fuck this up because
> there is no second chance for this. Especially not for Black and brown people.
> We have learned our lesson through the hundreds of years of segregation,
> oppression in this country, that there is no second chance for us. We either
> get it done the right way first or we have to live through a hundred years of
> Jim Crow. Or we have to live through a hundred years of Native American
> genocide. It is one of those things, it has been proven time and time again
> that we cannot sit on the sidelines and do this.

Framing Cannabis Reform

Many proponents of cannabis reform came to believe that framing
support for cannabis legalization in economic terms would help them
persuade more moderate or conservative voters to support their cause.[8]
Rachel, for example, told me, "If we're speaking to a more conservative
audience, we use arguments . . . [like] Colorado seeing millions of dollars
in tax revenue that can go back into our communities. . . . I think for more
conservative audiences, they generally respond more to the economic perspective of marijuana legalization." This perspective shaped the strategy of
many cannabis legalization ballot-measure campaigns. These campaigns
typically downplayed concerns about racism and mass incarceration in
their messaging, out of fears that such arguments might alienate voters
(Bender 2016, 692–95; Schlussel 2017, 904–19). Instead, they focused primarily on economic arguments, such as the potential benefits of new tax
revenue that will be generated by the cannabis industry (Aviram 2015,
78-97; Kaufman 2022).

But did this economic framing actually contribute to the success of
cannabis legalization campaigns? Social movement scholars have long
argued that the way issues are framed can have instrumental impact on

how those issues are perceived by different audiences (Benford and Snow 2000, 630). But others have found that framing has no discernable impact on the outcome of ballot-measure campaigns (Mello 2019). Indeed, in a few cases cannabis reform activists did successfully resist corporate influence, and they appear to have suffered no real electoral consequences for doing so.

In Michigan, for example, a group called the Michigan Responsibility Council developed a business-friendly proposal to legalize cannabis for adult use in 2016. The bill, which would have allowed a very small group of companies to control the entire cannabis industry in the state, was opposed by grassroots activists from the cannabis community. They formed their own organization, MI Legalize, which was able to help kill the bill. MI Legalize was unable to qualify its own more progressive legalization proposal for the ballot, however. National cannabis reform organizations advised them that if they wanted to succeed in 2018, they would need to earn the support of corporate donors. Terry, a longtime cannabis activist in Michigan, recalled that:

> After our 2016 failure, we enlisted the help of Marijuana Policy Project. . . . [They] dictated to us that we would include large corporate donors . . . which included tobacco and alcohol representatives. . . . When our volunteer coordinators . . . refused to support things like protected distributorships and ways in which they sought to mirror the alcohol industry with the cannabis industry, those corporate donors lost interest in supporting our bill. They realized they weren't going to receive the exclusivity that they had wanted. . . . Our movement suffered eventually financially because of their loss. But we got a much better program because they were not involved as deeply as they could have been in the drafting of the language. . . . We had a vision that they didn't share, and our vision was of a very consumer-centric program, which gave home cultivation a large allotment of cannabis and a large allotment of plants. And those were directly opposite of what the corporate goals had.

The Michigan campaign did suffer somewhat from a lack of corporate investments. The 2018 campaign in Michigan was one of the few instances where a pro cannabis legalization campaign was actually outspent by their opponents (see table 1). Despite this, voters in Michigan still overwhelmingly supported cannabis legalization.

Too much corporate support may actually be a liability for cannabis legalization campaigns. The most spectacular recent failure of a cannabis legalization campaign occurred in Ohio in 2015. Ohio's Issue 3 looked very similar to the business-friendly legalization proposal that local activists defeated in Michigan in 2016. It would have legalized cannabis in Ohio and given ten companies exclusive rights to legally grow, process, and sell cannabis in the state. The measure was written and placed on the ballot by a conservative business group representing the ten companies that would have been allowed to control Ohio's cannabis industry. It was widely panned by the cannabis community, who complained that it would create a monopoly for the big cannabis industry and it failed to generate widespread support. The bill's corporate donors poured more than $21.5 million into the campaign, but were still handily defeated 64–36—the largest margin of defeat for an adult-use cannabis legalization ballot measure ever (see table 1).

Given this, there does seem to be some recognition within the cannabis community that corporations were given too much control over legalization efforts in the past. Tamara reflected on the shifting trajectory of the movement, telling me:

> In [campaigns in] '13, '14, '15 so much of the conversation became dominated by typical economic incentives. Getting on the cover of *Forbes* magazine, and *Potrepreneur*, and *Gold Rush*, and so many things around "look at these new rich people we're making or people we're making even richer." And a lot of the core economic arguments were divorced from justice in ways that were fairly disturbing. But in the last . . . four years, I would say, a lot of the conversation has shifted to equity, and that's really exciting . . . and sort of embarrassing for me that we weren't focusing on that in 2012 nearly as much as we could have. I think that we didn't understand the ways that the economics of racial inequity in business at large in America was going to replicate itself in this area.

When states like Illinois and New York legalized cannabis in 2020 and 2021, activists made sure that social justice issues like criminal justice reform and racial equity featured prominently in the bill. As we shall see in the next chapter, however, even well-intentioned cannabis legalization bills contain loopholes that can be exploited.

The Inequity of Cannabis Legalization

> We are not past the prohibition here, we have legalization and prohibition at the same time. It's totally undeniable. . . . We have a complex, legal landscape. We have both illegality and legality.
> —Carl (cannabis activist)

The growing relationship between corporations and cannabis has changed the culture of the cannabis community and helped ease the passage of more business-friendly cannabis legalization bills. This has resulted in a system that distributes the benefits of cannabis legalization unevenly. Cannabis legalization has had enormous benefits for those who can adapt to this new corporate cannabis culture. But there are many in the cannabis community who do not fit comfortably in the business world. For most of these people, cannabis legalization has done little to improve their lives, and in some cases it has even made their situation worse.

Creating an Exclusive Cannabis Industry

Each state that has legalized cannabis for adult use has had to develop its own unique regulatory framework to govern this new industry. The absence of federal oversight in this area allows states to act as "laboratories of democracy" (Chemerinsky et al. 2015) and has generated quite a bit of innovation. It has also created a hodgepodge of different regulatory mechanisms that can be confusing to navigate and difficult to discuss comprehensively. No matter how they choose to organize their industry though, all of these states have one thing in common—they have all created cannabis industries that are overwhelmingly dominated by white business owners, most of whom had little relationship to cannabis prior to legalization.

Demographic data on the US cannabis industry is difficult to locate since most states do not provide that information publicly. But what we do know is discouraging for anyone who believes that cannabis legalization should be used to promote racial equity. Figure 1 shows the racial demographics of the cannabis industry in 2021 in three states that share

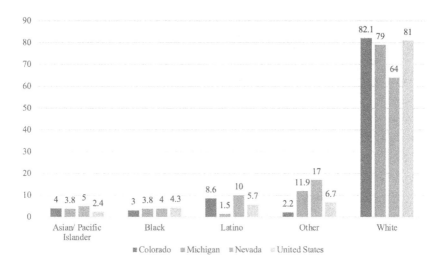

Figure 1. Percentage of Cannabis Business Owners by Race. *Source*: Compiled by author from the following sources: Colorado Department of Revenue 2022; Nevada Cannabis Compliance Board 2021; Michigan Regulatory Agency 2021; McVey 2017.

that data publicly (Colorado, Nevada, and Michigan), plus a widely cited national survey from 2017 that was conducted by the media outlet *Marijuana Business Daily*. This data indicates that white people are overrepresented, and people of color are dramatically underrepresented, among cannabis industry business owners relative to their population. Even so, it likely overstates the amount of diversity in the legal cannabis industry nationally.[9] A recent study conducted by the company Leafly, which did not disaggregate data based on ethnicity, estimated that only 1.2–1.7 percent of all cannabis business owners nationwide are Black (Barcott, Whitney, and Bailey 2021, 12–14).

   In Colorado white people account for 67.7% of the state's population, but they account for 82.1% of the state's cannabis industry owners and executives. In contrast, 21.8% of Coloradans identify as Latino, but only 8.6% of cannabis industry owners and executives in the state do. Only 4% of Coloradans identify as Black, but they are slightly underrepresented in the industry at just 3.1% of business owners. In Nevada only 48.2% of the state identifies as white, yet white people account for 64% of the state's cannabis industry owners and executives. In contrast 29.2% of Nevadans identify as Latino and 10.3% as Black, yet they only represent 10% and 4% of the state's cannabis industry owners and executives respectively. In Michigan, which has the newest industry of the three states in this sample, 61.6% of the population is white, yet white people account for 79% of industry owners and executives. In contrast, 17.4% of Michiganders identify as Black, and 18.7% as Latino, yet they only represent 3.8% and 1.5% of the state's cannabis owners and executives respectively (see fig. 1).

The lack of diversity amongst cannabis business owners and executives has been a huge disappointment for many longtime cannabis activists. Kimberly told me:

> The initial . . . idea of [cannabis legalization] was to start to undo some of the harms of the War on Drugs. . . . [Yet] I could count on one hand the number of business owners that are actually Black people. The majority of the industry in [my state], and I would daresay everywhere at this point, is white men. These were not the people that were targeted because of cannabis prohibition, and yet they are now benefiting from legalization. It's adding salt to the wound.

People like Kimberly have come to see cannabis legalization as a unique opportunity, not just to stop the War on Drugs from continuing to harm communities of color in the future, but also to repair some of the damage that was done to these communities in the past. Not only has cannabis legalization not done that, in many ways it has made the situation even worse.

This failure to create a licensing system that allows everyone who wants to participate in the legal cannabis industry to do so has consequences for real people. Todd has operated a cannabis dispensary in Southern California for nearly a decade. He operated in the state legally under California's medical cannabis statute. When California legalized cannabis for adult use in 2016, he sought to obtain a business license for his dispensary. But the city that he operated in declined to issue any licenses to cannabis businesses. This is a common experience for prospective cannabis business owners in legal cannabis states. Most of these states give municipalities the ability to "opt out" of legalization if they so choose. The vast majority of local governments have exercised that right, declining to allow cannabis businesses to operate in their jurisdiction. In California for example, more than six years after legalization, fewer than half of the state's cities and counties allowed cannabis businesses (California Department of Cannabis Control 2022). Similarly, in Michigan only about 9 percent of municipalities allowed legal cannabis in 2022 (Michigan Department of Treasury 2022). These local restrictions prevent entrepreneurs from opening business in their communities. Some have argued that they represent the biggest barrier to minority business owners entering the cannabis industry (Fertig 2020).

After being denied access to the legal industry, Todd made the difficult decision to continue operating in the illicit cannabis space, despite the legal risks of doing so. He is not alone. It is estimated that the illicit market still accounts for as much as 80 percent of the cannabis that is bought or sold in California (Demko and Nieves 2020). This experience of being locked out of the legal cannabis market has left Todd feeling frustrated, betrayed, and also misunderstood. Most assume that he has chosen to operate in the illicit market in order to avoid paying taxes, or because he does not want to operate according to the state's rules. The reality is more complicated. Todd explains:

> Most of us out here that are really doing their things right, want to be legal. . . . We'd like to do everything the way that the state wants it done. And we can do it, really easily. . . . We've all, in this illegal market, have been looking over our shoulder for so stinking long, you know? It's hard to even imagine the relief of knowing that you're totally legal, and that they're not going to do a damned thing to you. And that nothing's going to happen, and that you're doing everything right. It's what I strive for . . . that someday the laws are going to be changing, and I'd be able to do it legal. . . . [But] we can't get a license. So, we're doing the same thing, looking over our shoulder, hoping that we don't get pulled over or . . . something stupid happens, period. And they're over there saying, "Get legal." And we're going, "No, you can't get legal."

One of the main reasons that many want to legalize cannabis is to reduce the amount of people who are arrested for cannabis offenses. Yet, Todd's story shows that in many cases legal cannabis laws have actually had the opposite effect. Under California's medical cannabis statute Todd enjoyed some protections from arrest. Ironically, legalization has made him an outlaw again.

Legalization for Me, but Not for Thee

The inequities of cannabis legalization are not confined to the cannabis industry alone. Cannabis legalization has also impacted cannabis consumers in ways which mirror existing societal power dynamics. Most of my interviewees, even those who expressed disappointment with the way that legalization was carried out, reported feeling an increased sense of legitimacy and social acceptance as the cultural stigma around cannabis use has dissipated. For example, Charles told me:

> I have a fifty-three-year history of marijuana use. And the entire time I was breaking state, county, federal laws. And to use marijuana in my own backyard, and not be breaking at least state, county, or municipal laws was such a relief. To gain that kind of pain relief, anxiety relief, and then to not have any kind of fear associated with its use. That I'm breaking laws. That I'm a law breaker. It was a marvelous experience my first time. And it still continues to be a very good thing that I'm very grateful to be able to take advantage of.

Others reported a similar experience of relief once cannabis was legalized. Cecil, who had long kept his cannabis use private, in order to protect his professional reputation, told me that he felt more freedom to be candid about his relationship with cannabis after legalization.

> I just joined a [local] yacht club, which is a pretty conservative group. . . . My girlfriend immediately told people I was a marijuana lawyer, when I'm trying to think it's not going to be that socially acceptable, and just keep it low key. Well, everybody thinks it's really cool. . . . And so, I think the times they are a-changing. Now that we have legalization, people are willing to admit that they're consumers. . . . It's gone from tie-dye to suit and tie.

Typically, when people talk about the benefits of legalizing cannabis, they emphasize the potential for material gains such as reductions in arrest rates, or the ability to generate revenue from the cannabis industry. But, as these quotes show, legalizing cannabis does more than just give people the right to buy, sell, or use the drug. It also has constitutive impact on the identity of the people who participate in these activities. This is because, "[rights] do not merely entitle an individual to *do something*. . . . They also entitle each individual to *be someone*—to be recognized by others as a citizen, as a member of society, as an autonomous individual within the American democracy" (Engel and Munger 2003, 83). In this way, legalizing cannabis allows at least some members of the cannabis community to be recognized as responsible citizens who are deserving of rights.

For Charles and Cecil, both white men with professional careers, the relief that legalization brings them is mostly symbolic. Though they were "law breakers," during prohibition, the odds that they would actually suffer legal consequences for cannabis use were relatively slim. Indeed, despite decades of cannabis use and activism, neither of them had ever been incarcerated for a cannabis offense. For Black people, however, who despite reporting equal rates of use are still nearly four times more likely to be arrested for a cannabis offense than whites (ACLU 2020), the relief that comes from legalization is often both real and symbolic. Sara explains:

> I used to live in Virginia and it's scary . . . because Virginia [was at the time] one of the most strict states in the country [regarding cannabis use]. Moving to [an area] where it's basically legal and it's just a different feeling. You feel a lot more free. You're not worried about cops harassing you, even though they'll still harass you because they're cops. . . . I think, less fear means that people are happier. It means that people have less to worry about. They have less stress. They can enjoy their lives. . . . You don't have to worry about getting thrown in jail.

Though legalizing cannabis will not end police harassment, prevent the use of pretext stops, or even stop the police from making cannabis arrests, it does have the effect of making these fears a little less prominent for many, and that is meaningful.

But the symbolic benefits of cannabis legalization have not been distributed equally. Even in legal cannabis states there are still legal restrictions and policies that effectively exclude people with lower social status from being able to enjoy cannabis legally. Mindy, for example, told me:

> Weed is legal if you live in private housing, on private property in your back yard, only, maybe, kind of, sort of. But if you live in public housing, even if you have a prescription, you can't smoke in your house. There are still private apartment communities . . . that specifically say, "We don't care whether or not it's legal in your jurisdiction, our corporate office says no go, so you don't get to have it." . . . When I was trying to find a new apartment with my partner, we went through several different apartments trying to find anyone that would give us an exception for medical [cannabis]. . . . To make it safe, I always ask about . . . noncombustibles. And even then, people are skeptical, or not willing to lease to you.

These restrictions are particularly burdensome for people of color, who face a much higher likelihood of being arrested for a cannabis offense, even in states where cannabis is now legal. Eric told me, "People think, 'Oh, it's legal now. I can do whatever I want. I can walk down the street and smoke it like it's a cigarette.' No. No, you can't. And then people still don't know that even though it's legal to carry [cannabis], but if you're not a medical card holder, it has to be in your trunk. . . . So, it was little things like that that is why people of color are still being arrested."

Even when cannabis is being used in legally permissible ways, racial and gender stereotypes still prevent many cannabis users from less privileged backgrounds from enjoying the same symbolic benefits of legalization that people like Charles or Cecil received. Julie told me:

> There's definitely a stigma. Yeah, definitely a stigma. . . . To go into some of the dispensaries or to go to purchase some of the products, it's just not a good look for a woman my age walking into one of them. . . . I'm an active parent. I've participated in the Booster's Club and all of those kind of things. Somebody seeing me, you know, they're gonna shake their finger at me and wonder what kind of a mom I am. That still happens today. It still happens today. People, medical patients are losing their kid over this stuff. It's crazy.

This suggest that as cannabis is legalized it shifts from being regulated exclusively by police officers and the criminal justice system to being controlled by a mix of formal bureaucratic regulations, backed by both criminal and civil statutes, as well as informal social norms. As a result, legalization may have the paradoxical effect of actually increasing the mechanisms the state has for controlling and regulating cannabis. Combating these forms of control is, in many ways, even more difficult for cannabis activists, because they are less visible, and thus more difficult to articulate, than cannabis prohibition was.

THREE

Creating Docile Bodies

Legal Cannabis and the Carceral State

At first glance, legalizing cannabis would seem to represent a reduction in state power. What was once a prohibited activity that the state attempted to eradicate through arrests and incarcerations is now permitted. Most states that have legalized cannabis have seen dramatic reductions in cannabis arrests and businesses are now making millions selling a once-illicit substance. Yet a closer look at how the cannabis industry is regulated reveals that, instead of giving up its power over cannabis, the state has merely exchanged one mechanism of controlling this industry for another, more subtle, and much more effective one. This chapter shows how the state has used its power to regulate and tax cannabis to consolidate its control over the drug, bringing a marketplace that it has been unable to control through prohibition alone to heel through legalization. In this way carceral power is extended beyond the walls of the prison into all aspects of social life (Foucault 1978, 293–308).

The ability to regulate and tax economic activity is one of the most powerful tools governments have for controlling their citizenry. As John Marshall once famously intoned, "the power to tax involves the power to destroy" (*McCulloch v. Maryland* 1819, 431). Legal cannabis states have all used their newfound powers to regulate and tax cannabis to create a legal cannabis industry that operates according to their terms. Those who wish to participate in the legal cannabis space must acquire the proper licenses, pay the required fees, and comply with a dizzying array of rules and regulations. Some are willing and able to comply with these new requirements, but most are not. These regulations act as barriers to entry, preventing many people from being able to participate in the legal cannabis industry, and reproducing status quo power structures. As a result, the same predominantly Black and brown communities that were most adversely impacted by the War on Drugs are also the ones most likely to find themselves shut out of the legal cannabis industry.

These new regulations are justified by the logic of the market, which makes them seem more legitimate, and helps obscure the crucial role that the state plays in supporting them. It may seem a slight improvement to have one's dream of running a cannabis business destroyed by a form letter notifying them that "your application for a cannabis business license has been denied," than by a police raid. But neither option is desirable. Though the more bureaucratic rejection appears less violent, this is largely an illusion. As Robert Cover reminds us, "legal interpretation takes place in a field of pain and death" (1986, 1601). People do not passively follow the state's ever-changing rules governing cannabis because they think that it is the right thing to do—they do it because they know that if they do not do so they will likely end up on the receiving end of state-sanctioned violence. Violators face the possibility of being fined, having their property seized, even being incarcerated.

Those who are unable to enter the legal cannabis space are forced to either leave the cannabis trade entirely or continue operating in the illicit marketplace after legalization, even though doing so risks arrest. Though cannabis arrests have declined since legalization, they have not gone away. Thousands of people are still being arrested each year for cannabis offenses in legal cannabis states. These arrests have been targeted primarily at communities of color. The gap between Black and white arrest rates for cannabis offenses has actually increased in many legal cannabis states post legalization (ACLU 2020, 36). This shows that legalizing cannabis should be understood less as a transition away from the policies of mass incarceration and more as an attempt to redirect how police power is used in order to better serve the state's interest in controlling the cannabis trade.

Barriers to Entry

> One of the most unfortunate things to come from legalization, is that the very communities that were harmed by prohibition have not been provided opportunity to benefit from legalization. That's come, in part, because of the realities of the business world, who has access to the resources, financial and otherwise, that are needed to establish businesses. And partly because the very people that were targeted by the War on Drugs are at times systematically excluded from the industry because of their criminal records.
> —Bruce (cannabis activist)

People decide to engage in social movement activism for a variety of, often idiosyncratic, reasons. Still, nearly all the activist that I spoke with for this project cited the need for criminal justice reform as a primary motivation. What excites many of these activists about cannabis legalization is that it provides a rare opportunity not just to help end the racist legacy of the War on Drugs, but also to do something to repair the damage that was done to communities of color by the policies of mass incarceration. Sara summed up the feelings of many activists when she told me:

> We [have to] take seriously the idea of repairing. It's not just about moving forward. . . . It's about [helping] the people who have had a marijuana-related conviction on their record for years. . . . People who are locked out of employment. People who were basically put into cyclical poverty because they had to check the convict box. Without . . . giving restitution to those people, I don't feel that legalization could ever really fulfill a whole aspect of repairing what the injustices were. . . . [And] it's not just people themselves that have been harmed. It's their families, it's their communities, it's their loved ones. Everybody surrounding them have been harmed.

If cannabis legalization is to function as reparations, then the proceeds from this new industry must flow to the communities that were the most negatively affected by the War on Drugs. Perhaps the easiest way to do this is to enable Black and brown entrepreneurs to successfully enter into, and profit from, the legal cannabis industry. Indeed, that was the goal that many activists, and even some lawmakers, had in mind when they first legalized cannabis. But this goal has proven more difficult to accomplish than many of these people imagined.

Expensive Licenses, Complicated Application Processes

Neoliberal economic theory reveres the "free market" as the best mechanism for promoting innovation and generating economic growth (Mudge 2008). Yet, gaining entry into the legal cannabis industry is anything but free.[1] The application fee for a cannabis business license alone typically costs tens of thousands of dollars. Even if an applicant does have the necessary funds to pay this fee, they still need to be able to fill out a lengthy, and complicated, application form, full of technical jargon, and provide a detailed business proposal.[2] This process is so complicated that most successful applicants have to hire an attorney and/or a business consultant to assist them with the application, adding further expense. This means that applicants can expect to pay $100,000 or more in most states just to apply for a chance to obtain a cannabis business license. Julie, a longtime cannabis activist in California, explained:

> There's a city out here who charged over $40,000 for an application fee, and the lowest one I've seen is just under $8,000. . . . And that doesn't include [attorney fees] . . . an attorney would charge you about 40 to 50 grand to fill out an application for you. That's only your local [application]. That's not even your state . . . [and] you're throwing that money in there just to spin the wheel. . . . You've gotta put that money in and you might not get a [license].

The high cost and level of technical expertise required to successfully apply for a cannabis business license puts those who have spent most of their life working in the illicit industry, where such requirements do not exist, at a disadvantage. Julie told me, "People that have worked in the black market generally don't have a basic business knowledge. So, you're asking him to jump through all of these hoops versus somebody who's had his own insurance company or his own trucking company. . . . He knows all of these things. . . . The chances that they're gonna get a permit or a license is slim to none."

The high cost of procuring a cannabis license is especially burdensome because federal law prohibits financial institutions from lending money to cannabis businesses. This means that those looking to enter the cannabis industry must often find a way to self-finance their venture. Many have gone to extreme measures to do so. Jody, who runs a cannabis business in Washington, told me:

> Banks won't do loans. . . . [So] I called all of my credit cards and I told them I was buying a BMW and I wanted the points instead of paying interest to a car company, so I had them all up to ridiculous rates. I took second mortgages on both my homes, I took a second mortgage on my mother's home. . . . I knew that we needed to make sure that we had as much capital available to us from day one because once anybody knew what business I was in, no bank's going to lend to me.

The need to self-finance a cannabis business is particularly burdensome for people of color, who typically have less access to capital. The average white family in the United States has eight times the wealth of the average Black family, and five times the wealth of the average Latino family (Bhutta et al. 2020). This means that is harder for people of color to find the money that they need to successfully navigate the licensing process, let alone to cover the start-up costs of a new business venture. Catherine, who owns a cannabis business in Washington, explains:

> Because of federal status of marijuana, any kind of financing was really hard to find. . . . A lot of people funded themselves with their real estate money. . . . African American folks are less likely to own real estate . . . I know quite a few people who had paid off properties, and they took out mortgages on their properties and used that money to fund their marijuana build-out. I myself cashed out a 401K and I sold stock options, and then we had a small family inheritance that came through around that time, too, that helped fund our startup. But if you don't have access to that money somewhere, it's pretty hard to get into the industry.

Those who cannot afford to self-finance their venture must either give up on their dream of operating a legitimate cannabis business or find a corporate sponsor who is willing to bankroll them. These partnerships are, in theory, mutually beneficial relationships. The corporation gains someone with valuable experience working in the illicit or medical cannabis industry, and the applicant gains access to the financial resources and business expertise of their corporate sponsor. Both Colorado and California have established incubator programs designed to facilitate these types of collaborations. But these partnerships are often not as beneficial to the applicant as they may seem. Many of these contracts are written in ways that give the applicants no real decision-making power over business matters, tightly limit their share of the profits, or include "buy-out" clauses that require them to sell their share of the business if certain, often unrealistic, benchmarks are not met (Bricken 2018). Eric, a cannabis activist in Illinois, told me:

> There has been reports of a lot of [multistate operators] are going to individuals who applied for licenses and gave them deals and they'll help set it up and help them operate the thing. But the moment they're not profitable, they would just take over. These buy-out clauses or just asking people, offering them $25,000 to be on the applications, it's just front people. . . . They are preying on individuals who never had anything, to cheat them out of a great opportunity.

These applicants often know that the contract they are signing is problematic, but many feel like they have no choice but to sign these predatory business deals anyway. Jacob, a lawyer and cannabis activist in Illinois explained, "They're not going to have extra money to go hire an attorney and pay them . . . $500 an hour to review [their] contract. . . . A lot of them were in positions where they continue to work with these folks, or don't apply for a license at all. So, many just signed wherever they were told."

The fact that the legal cannabis industry has replicated the same patterns of racial privilege seen in other segments of the US economy is regrettable, but it is not particularly surprising. As law professor Angela Harris tells us, "Racial subjugation is not a special application of capitalist processes, but rather central to how capitalism operates" (2021, vii). Racism is baked into our capitalist economic system, which relies on the exitance of a permanent underclass of labor to be exploited. In the United States, as in much of the western world, that underclass has always been disproportionately comprised of racial and ethnic minorities (Jenkins and Leroy 2021). One of the more insidious parts of this system is the way in which the economic logic of the market is used to frame these barriers to entry as race neutral, merit-based restrictions. Prospective business owners are not rejected because they are Black or Latino, they are rejected because they lack the required funds or necessary technical expertise. This ignores the ways in which these economic expectations replicate status quo power structures, and it elides the state's role in creating these rules in the first place. After all, it was not some "invisible hand" that created an overly complicated application process for cannabis business licenses or decided to charge a $40,000 application fee—these were deliberately designed government policies!

If we are serious about creating a cannabis industry that does not perpetuate existing racial inequities, then the state needs to provide resources to help overcome these structural disadvantages. Instead, most states that have legalized cannabis have created rules and regulations that exacerbate them. Those who support racial equity in the legal cannabis industry have pushed for two sets of changes designed to reverse this trend and help more people of color enter the industry: the expungement of criminal records and the development of social equity programs. These ideas are well-intentioned, but they have proven difficult to implement successfully.

Criminal Records Restrictions

Criminal record restrictions are one of the biggest barriers to entry preventing many people of color, especially those with a history of working in the illicit cannabis industry, from obtaining a cannabis business license. Having a criminal conviction on one's record operates as negative credential, preventing them from exercising a host of rights and privileges that other citizens enjoy (Pager 2007). Jacquelyn, a drug reform activist, explained that "across the country there are a little over 50,000 legal restrictions for people with criminal convictions, so really concrete barriers for moving on with their life, getting jobs, getting education, getting loans, getting housing, being able to participate in your kids' school activities." These criminal records restrictions disproportionately impact people of color, since they are far more likely than white people to be arrested for a cannabis offense.

It seems obvious that people who were previously convicted of something that the state now deems permissible should not have to continue suffering the consequences of that conviction. Yet, none of the early cannabis legalization states allowed for the expungement of past cannabis offenses initially (Berman 2018). This omission sparked outrage from activists, who successfully pressured lawmakers to adopt expungement provisions. Today, most legal cannabis states do include some mechanism for expunging at least low-level cannabis offenses.[3] Despite these changes however, the vast majority of people with cannabis convictions still never get their records expunged and will struggle to reintegrate into the legitimate economy as a result.

Byron is a Latino cannabis activist. His father was incarcerated for a drug offense when he was a child. He was raised by his mother and has no memory of ever seeing his father outside of the walls of a prison. As an adolescent, Byron had a few run-ins with the law and ended up with a criminal conviction for a cannabis offense, "plus a few other things." He learned from these youthful mistakes however, becoming an entrepreneur, obtaining a college degree, and involving himself in his community by engaging in social movement activism. In spite of this, his criminal record prevented him from working in the cannabis industry:

> I applied for [work in] a dispensary. The managers were super awesome. They loved me. I was right on board. Then they did a CORI check. . . . It's a database . . . of all the criminal records [of] anybody . . . that is a United States citizen. . . . That was one of the barriers. I couldn't proceed and work in the dispensary and then when I sought out how to do an expungement, obviously I [was] a college student so I don't have the capital or the financial resources to pay a lawyer. Nor were there any type of other services that I found . . . that were able to help me through the expungement process.

What is perhaps most remarkable about this story is that Byron lives in a state that has taken measures to help people like him enter the legal cannabis industry. His state does not automatically exclude those with criminal records from working in the cannabis industry, and it does allow for the expungement of criminal records for most low-level cannabis offenses. Yet, Byron received no guidance on how to navigate these resources. As a result, he was unaware of some of the programs that might have been available to him and found it difficult to make use of the resources that he did know about.

Byron's experience is a common one for those who have a criminal record. Studies show that less than 10 percent of people who are eligible to have their criminal records expunged will successfully petition to do so (Prescott and Starr 2020; Berman 2018, 311–312). This is because the process of getting one's criminal record expunged is extremely complicated, time intensive, and often expensive. Jacquelyn told me:

Understanding your own criminal conviction history and your rap sheet is really complicated. A lot of people don't know that they're eligible. . . . The process to actually get your record cleared, even if you know you're eligible, it's complicated and it can take a long time. So, people have to take time off work to go to court to meet with attorneys. Oftentimes it requires money to do, either by hiring attorneys or through court fees that are required. So, those are the big barriers that people face to getting a record cleared through the petition-based process.

These challenges are not felt by everyone equally. Those with economic means can afford to pay an attorney to help guide them through the process and can more easily take time off from work to attend hearings. They also tend to live in more affluent communities, which typically have fewer expungements to process, and more resources to dedicate to processing them. This means that the expungement process moves much faster for them than for those who live in large municipalities, where overwhelmed courts often take years to fully process expungements. Bruce, a cannabis activist and scholar, explains how these dynamics make expunging one's criminal record particularly difficult for people of color:

The people who are most likely to have been arrested for cannabis . . . are more likely to be those that are politically, socially and economically marginalized . . . less likely to afford legal counsel to help them go through this process. And so those people that perhaps need help the most or need the record suspensions the most are the least likely to actually be able to go about getting those themselves without some kind of aid or resources.

Legal Aid societies, law schools, and activists with legal training often try to assist people navigating the expungement process by offering free clinics and legal advice. But these programs can only provide relief to the small number of people who are actively looking to expunge their criminal record. A more effective solution might be to move away from a petition-based expungement process altogether, toward one that is proactive and automatic. Code for America, a nonprofit advocacy organization that seeks to use technology to make government run more efficiently, has developed software called "Clear My Record," which enables local governments to identify and then automatically expunge the criminal records of everyone who is eligible. This system was first tested in five California counties in 2019, where it helped clear more than 75,000 cannabis convictions (Ciaramella 2019). Automatic expungement is no panacea. It is typically only available for those with a single misdemeanor cannabis offense, and there are questions about whether these small pilot programs can be effectively scaled up. Still, widespread adoption of automatic expungement has the potential to help hundreds of thousands of Americans recover from the effects of a cannabis conviction.

Social Equity Programs

As difficult as it has been to address criminal record restrictions, designing government programs that can help poor people of color overcome structural disadvantages and gain entry into the legal cannabis industry has proven to be even more challenging. Indeed, until very recently states did not even try. Illinois, which legalized cannabis in 2020, was the first state to explicitly build "social equity" provisions into its cannabis legalization bill. The state placed strict limits on the number of cannabis business licenses available, gave preference to qualified equity applicants during the application process, and provided them with technical assistance.[4] It also established a cannabis business development fund, which provides low-interest business loans to equity applicants who would otherwise struggle to obtain the necessary capital. Finally, the state mandated that 25 percent of all revenue generated from cannabis taxes and fees be invested in communities that were disproportionately impacted by the War on Drugs. Many states have since followed Illinois' lead, implementing equity programs that provide technical assistance to qualified applicants, reduce or eliminate their application fees, help them obtain financing, and expedite their application review process.[5]

These equity provisions sound promising. Illinois' bill was widely celebrated at the time as the most progressive cannabis reform law ever passed (Chander 2022), and New York's social equity provisions are set to be even more robust (Schroyer 2022). So far, however, the results have been disappointing. It took nearly two years for the state of Illinois to issue its first business license to an equity applicant.[6] In the meantime, Illinois' legal cannabis industry was completely controlled by the companies that had been operating in the medical cannabis space previously. Almost all of these companies were large multistate operators backed by wealthy white ownership groups (Schuba 2020). According to a study commissioned by the state of Illinois that was later leaked to the media, less than 2 percent of cannabis dispensary owners in Illinois were Black or Latino during this time period (Fourcher 2021). More recently, the state has begun granting a small number of equity licenses, but despite this, the Illinois cannabis industry is still overwhelmingly controlled by large multistate operators backed by wealthy white ownership groups (McCoppin 2021). Similar problems have plagued the rollout of social equity programs in states like California and Massachusetts as well (Orenstein 2020).

One reason that Illinois' equity program has struggled has to do with how the state chose to define an equity applicant. Lawmakers were advised that using explicitly race-based classifications would likely run into legal hurdles, given Supreme Court jurisprudence in the area of affirmative action. In order to avoid these legal challenges, they defined a "social equity applicant" using race-neutral terms. An ownership group could initially qualify as an equity applicant in Illinois in one of three ways: (1) if 51 percent of their owners have resided for at least five of the last ten years in an area that the state considers to have been disproportionately impacted by the War on Drugs, (2) if 51 percent of owners have an expungable drug arrest on their criminal record or have a close relative who does, or (3) by committing to hire at least ten employees and ensuring that at least 51 percent of those employees would qualify as social equity applicants.[7] Other states have similarly sought to define equity applicants in race-neutral terms (Kinley2023).

The state's definition of "equity applicant" seems reasonable, but it ended up containing loopholes that were relatively easy to manipulate in practice. Race-blind definitions of diversity often undermine attempts to provide targeted benefits to people who have been harmed by racist policies like the War on Drugs (Berrey 2015). Jacob told me:

> There were a lot of different ways that companies, that weren't really the intended beneficiaries of the social equity program, could benefit from it. . . . Being 51% owned by someone that lives in a disproportionately impacted area. That sounds great . . . on paper, but . . . because of the nature of gentrification, and the way that neighborhoods aren't always economically, completely segregated. There are folks that are really wealthy white men, who live in disproportionately impacted areas. . . . They can qualify first for social

equity status. . . . Being 51% owned by someone with an expugnable cannabis arrest or conviction. That could be . . . a George Bush [type] social equity advocate. He got pulled over, arrested for DUIs and cocaine. . . . Or, if your company is 51% owned by a close relative of someone with a cannabis, expugnable. . . . Again, it can be a billionaire who has a son . . . and he gets arrested for cannabis. . . . Now, the rich billionaire dad is a social equity applicant. We've seen some examples of something like that.

Activists in Illinois had particular scorn for the state's "promise to hire" clause, which proved to be the most easily manipulated social equity provision. Jeffrey told me, "There's a reason that's called the 'slave-master clause.' There's no other way that we can frame that other than that. That is sharecropping in 2021. . . . That's just such a glaring oversight, that it's just welcoming people to take advantage of." Indeed, the promise to hire clause received so much criticism that it was removed from subsequent rounds of the Illinois cannabis licensing lottery, but not before a number of companies were able to benefit from it (Schuba 2021a). As a result, the majority of the licenses that were eventually granted to "equity applicants" in Illinois did not end up going to people of color (McCoppin 2021).

The failures of these social equity programs have left many cannabis activists and people of color feeling a deep sense of frustration and betrayal. Sara put it this way:

I feel like equity is a buzzword right now. . . . Diversity is cool now, right. We're marketing diversity. . . . Throwing around equity, and we care about diversity, and these are diversity hires and blah, blah, blah. It's marketing. . . . It is just a buzzword to make black people and brown people feel better about waiting for things that aren't ever going to come. . . . Black people have been fed the same line of shit . . . saying, "we'll get to you later." And that's never what it is. It's basically, "Get out of our way. Let us do this and then maybe we'll give you a few breadcrumbs later."

Jacob, who is also Black, shared similar frustrations, "It's just infuriating sometimes. To see certain folks make tons of money just because of their proximity to power and wealth, and American privilege, it's infuriating. And that's caused . . . a lot of stress in my life. I'm like, 'I'm super qualified.' And companies in the neighborhood are still struggling to find my place in the industry . . . and other folks like me." Guy was even more despondent: "Legalization for me has . . . been a hurtful thing to watch.

It's just been hurtful to watch how the Black community's been excluded, how the Black community has not been given true information on how to get into the industry, how to sustain in the industry. . . . Legal cannabis, man, is really a trick to me."

Consolidating the Cannabis Industry

> I see so many people who have invested . . . their life savings into [the] pursuit of their dreams in this industry and have gone bankrupt. . . . I think that that is one of the sad stories about legalization . . . that some of the folks who worked so hard under such hard circumstances before legalization, and tried to make that transition, have been some of the ones to suffer the most, and not see the dividends from it.
> —Ernest (cannabis activist)

As hard as it is to gain entry to the legal cannabis industry, running a profitable cannabis business once you get there might be even harder. The media has frequently portrayed the cannabis industry as a "green rush" with enormous profit potential (see, for example, Barcott 2017). The reality, however, is much different. Most cannabis business owners struggle to remain profitable and many fail. A recent survey conducted by the National Cannabis Industry Association found that 58 percent of all cannabis businesses in the United States are not currently profitable (Whitney 2022). Jody, who owns a cannabis business in Washington, told me:

> The legal market, it's the hardest thing I've ever done. I thought, "We're educated, we've had small businesses before, we've grown cannabis before." Like, I thought that this was a frickin' low-risk shoe-in. And instead, it is hands down the hardest thing I've ever done. . . . "Start your own business," they said. "Write your own hours," they said. . . . My husband and I went without a paycheck for four years. Not one. And now we make minimum wage as CEO and COO.

Another Washington-based cannabis business owner echoed those thoughts, telling me, "There's about 20 companies that consistently do above a million dollars a month. Then there's all the rest of us. We're at a fraction of that . . . the state's the only one cashing in on this gig."

These difficulties are not felt by everyone equally. Those with prior business experience and more access to capital have an easier time weathering such a challenging business environment. Smaller, more independent operators, however, who often have less legitimate business experience and far fewer resources struggle to survive. Minority-owned cannabis businesses are particularly vulnerable to these challenges. Though 58 percent of all cannabis business are either losing money or breaking even, 67.8 percent of minority-owned cannabis businesses are not currently profitable (Whitney 2022).

Fluid Regulatory Environment Strains Businesses

One reason that so many cannabis businesses have struggled is that legal cannabis is one of the most highly regulated products on the market. The evidence of this regulation is visible to anyone who enters a dispensary today. Security guards and security cameras are ubiquitous, expensive seed-to-sale tracking devices carefully monitor the movement of cannabis products, strict rules prohibit public consumption, and regulations on marketing and packaging carefully dictate how products are to be stored, displayed, and advertised. Regulations are an inevitable, and in many cases desirable, aspect of any well-run industry.[8] But a number of observers have noted that the cannabis industry is showing signs of being overregulated (Walsh 2020; Kary 2021). Such overregulation would be difficult for any industry to handle, but it is particularly burdensome for cannabis, which has a long history of being completely unregulated. Ruth, who grew cannabis for the illicit and quasi-legal medical cannabis markets before making the transition to the tightly regulated adult-use cannabis industry, explained:

> Coming from no regulations to over-the-moon regulations has not been easy; it's taken everything we've got mentally and physically and financially. . . . There is so many more hoops to jump and costs to cover and competition and regulatory ridiculousness that makes the regulated market a whole lot more complicated and uncomfortable than the unregulated market. . . . Packaging and labeling regulations, camera regulations, how we deal with our waste, what products we can and cannot sell. . . . Now we've got labor to gram it out, weigh it up, package it, heat seal it, all the costs of the packaging, the stickers, labels, all of that.

Keeping up with all of these rules and regulations requires a considerable investment of time and money—something that is typically in short supply when you are opening a small business.

Since cannabis is a new industry, these rules are constantly changing, making things even more complicated. Jody told me:

> The regular rules change all the time. In Washington State, last December there were seven Board Interim Policies [BIP], which are basically like emergency rules. . . . To have that many BIPs that are suddenly changing rules immediately is impossible to keep up on. When you do it on a shoestring budget, because we have [self-] funded everything. . . . You just can't buy packaging on an economic scale, or machinery, because you don't know if it's going to be outdated in six months, if they're suddenly going to change a rule and you're screwed. And that stuff is constant. It happens all the time.

This puts a tremendous burden on business owners. First, they have to work just to keep abreast of these changes. Then they have to invest resources in compliance. Finally, they must decide when and how to push back against regulations that they deem to be excessive. This would be taxing for any company, but it is particularly burdensome for small independent operators. They do not have the budget to hire lobbyists to influence the regulatory process on their behalf and can ill afford the lost revenue that complying with new regulations requires.

In addition to government regulations, cannabis business owners must also deal with a social environment in which cannabis is still highly stigmatized by many. Regulatory requirements are often weaponized against cannabis business owners by neighbors who would rather not have a cannabis business operating in their locality (Garriott 2020, 1008–14). As a result, many cannabis business owners have experienced difficulties acquiring properly zoned and compliant property for their business. Ruth told me:

> We busted our butt trying to find property that we could buy that was in a properly zoned area. . . . We found a ten-acre piece up in [a rural] county and bought it. . . . The citizenship went into overdrive trying to stop us. . . . After lots of citizen fear mongering, the county council reversed their [zoning] decision. . . . The only reason why we're still here is because we could put in building permits . . . and they had already been approved. So, we got grandfathered in under the old zoning.

And Jody said:

> I checked . . . to make sure that the location that we found was okay. . . . After we signed the fifteen-year lease, the Liquor and Cannabis Board . . . denied our location because we're next door to a Christian religious cheerleading camp and the rules say you have to be a thousand feet away from rec. centers. . . . So even though we had done everything correctly, we were hit with this right off the bat. . . . The fact that this cheerleader was worried about our risk to her youth. . . . You could see that that propaganda, that reefer madness that was continuing on. . . . We ended up winning that situation, but it put us months off.

In both of these cases, the business owner was able to successfully defeat these zoning challenges, but doing so cost time and money, and caused a considerable amount of stress and anxiety. Many are not so lucky.

This shows how the regulatory power of the state intersects with lingering societal stigma toward cannabis, to make life difficult for cannabis business owners. Even when business owners make a good faith effort to comply with things like zoning restrictions, they are often thwarted by property owners, citizens, or local politicians, who interpret these statutes broadly in order to fight against cannabis. The rules governing this industry may seem like neutral zoning restrictions, but examples like these show that the cultural stigma around cannabis has not gone away post-legalization. Instead, these moral logics have become entrenched in the regulatory system where, obscured by bland legalese, they become considerably more difficult to identify and combat.

Steep Learning Curve for Those Without Experience

Those with prior business expertise have a considerable advantage in such a competitive regulatory environment. Ruth runs a cannabis business with her husband in Washington. They successfully transitioned from the illicit market to the legal cannabis industry, and after years of struggle are now making a small profit. When I asked Ruth if she thought her background in the illicit cannabis industry had been helpful, she demurred. Instead, she credited their prior experience running a construction business as the key to their success. "We've been in business for decades. We came in knowing we had to pay the taxes, and we had to pay payroll taxes.

We came in understanding how to do that sort of stuff, but a lot of people came in not understanding that."

Most of the people looking to transition from the illicit to the legal cannabis industry are not so lucky. They may have considerable experience with cannabis, but they are accustomed to operating in an unregulated environment where things like writing a business plan, paying taxes, or making payroll are unnecessary. Michael explained:

> The idea that these people who have suffered the most should be given first in line, it sounds good on paper and I support the concept . . . [but] the question is . . . can the government devise some system where you can give these guys who've spent four years in prison for marijuana an advantage over a regular person? . . . It's one thing . . . to sell this stuff out of your car, off the sidewalk, in school, whatever, it's a completely different, obviously, environment than opening up a storefront, getting your business license, having employees, filling out 1099s and paying your bills on time and working the cash register. . . . It's a whole different skillset.

The correlation between prior business experience and success in the legal cannabis industry is so high that even many activists who support social equity have cautioned against lowering barriers to entry. Jody told me, "I totally believe in [social equity]. But they're like, 'Give them licenses.' I'm like, 'Why? So they can fail?' That's a horrible idea. . . . To just hand out licenses without really addressing some of the bigger issues around social equity . . . it's going to set people up for failure. And . . . I don't want to see a social equity program like that."

This lack of business experience is a real problem for many people who are trying to gain a foothold in the legal cannabis industry. But putting too much emphasis on it ignores the state's role in creating a business environment that works to the disadvantage of those who had been operating in the illicit industry previously. Worse, it recasts these failures as the legitimate product of individual moral flaws. Harriet told me, "Dealing with government regulations of course was not going to be our strength, being an underground and unregulated populous. We were quickly denigrated, 'under capitalized, under knowledgeable, under experienced,' and most of the folks who had been medical providers are now out of market." These criticisms are particularly resonant, because they align with existing stereotypes of those in the cannabis community as lazy, stupid, or unprofessional.

Not everyone who lacks relevant experience is denigrated for it, however. Most successful businesses owners do not have personal expertise sufficient to manage all aspects of their business. Indeed, many people who came to the legal cannabis industry from the business sector had no previous experience with cannabis at all. Yet, most of them had the financial resources required to acquire that expertise from others, whereas equity applicants do not. Jacob explained:

> I still sort of see everything as going back to access to capital because a lot of the operators right now, they didn't know anything about [business] either. They just had the money to go find the person that did. That's part of the name of the game, and most of these folks that are running companies now were not growing weed in their basement or in the regulated/unregulated market . . . they went and found somebody that did, and made them an employee.

This shows how wealth is often used as a signifier for worthiness in our capitalist economic system (Goldberg 2007; Bridges 2017). Wealthy people have the ability to move into new industries, like cannabis, without having any prior experience, and be taken seriously as responsible business owners who are deserving of these new opportunities. People who come from less economically privileged backgrounds cannot do the same. Their lack of business experience is not seen as a temporary barrier to be overcome, but as a fatal flaw, indicating that they lack the required talent, or are not industrious enough to succeed.

These differences have less to do with ability, and more to do with proximity to wealth and privilege, giving some people an inherent advantage that they did little to earn. Many cannabis activists believe the state has a moral responsibility to do more to level the playing field, particularly because government policies like mass incarceration have exacerbated these inequities. Eric, for example, said:

> If you never ran a business before, it's going to be difficult for you. But that's where there should have been training, classes on how to run a dispensary and things like that for these equity applicants. There should have been education, Business 101. How to set up their business, how to run your business, how to do your payroll. These things should have been provided. . . . Some of these people who have been incarcerated for [cannabis] in our community are undereducated, families torn apart. At some point, we have to look out for

these people. We can't continue to let the same old people monopolize every industry that opens.

Instead of acknowledging these factors, state actors have too often placed the blame for the failure of these cannabis businesses squarely on the shoulders of "underqualified" individual owners. In this way the state evades all responsibility for creating the conditions under which so many of these businesses have failed, and for not assisting business owners in their attempt to navigate this system. As a result, those in the cannabis community are denigrated for not having the proper expertise to succeed in this business, and the corporate takeover of the cannabis industry becomes a fait accompli.

Small Operators Struggle to Compete

The challenges of this business environment give large multistate operators a decided advantage over small independently owned cannabis businesses. The smaller operators who do succeed typically do so not by competing directly with the bigger players but by filling a niche in the market, such as growing premium "craft cannabis." Kenneth and his business partner had no prior business experience and only $150,000 in capital when they opened their small five-acre cannabis farm. When I talked with Kenneth, they had been running the business for a little over five years and were mostly successful. They survived with limited resources, in an extremely competitive business environment, by using small-scale, environmentally sustainable agricultural techniques to grow premium cannabis for the wholesale market. Still, he listed a number of major challenges facing small operators like them:

> The challenges have been . . . us competing with [large corporations] . . . who have the commercialization capacity and resources to blow out the retail market. That literally, there were years where we couldn't even get on the phone with a buyer. Where they would just say, "We're just not buying flower right now." . . . The threshold just to get into retail has been yet another significant challenge for us, especially as the smallest of the farms, the most craft cannabis. I think as the market has unfolded people have wanted cheap weed, and our business model doesn't really allow for us to have the smallest

canopy, the highest quality flower, the most craft tended to, and then to sell it for the cheapest. That's just not how that's going to work for us.

Small independent operators like Kenneth may be able to survive with shrewd business strategies, and more than a little luck, but narrow profit margins and limited opportunities for growth will always leave them vulnerable to fluctuations in the market. Even when they are financially solvent, the stress of running a small business under these circumstances drives many out of the legal industry. Indeed, when I last talked with Kenneth, he and his partner were in the process of selling their operation.

When business owners like Kenneth tire of dealing with these challenges, large operators are often eager to purchase their businesses at bargain prices. This leads to increased consolidation of the cannabis industry. If current trends continue, the cannabis market is likely to develop in ways similar to the alcohol industry. A few large operators will dominate the market with cheap mass-produced products, leaving independent operators to fight over the smaller craft cannabis sector (Hoban 2021). Still, many activists are hopeful that developing more niche markets will help create a more equitable cannabis industry. Jeffrey told me, "Corporate consolidation has hit every single industry in the United States. I don't expect cannabis to be any different . . . but if we can carve out . . . a portion of the industry that is really sustainable and independent from these big players, that would be a victory in my eyes."

Some activists even see benefits to corporate consolidation. Ruben, a cannabis activist in Nevada, pointed out that, from the perspective of many cannabis consumers, the corporate consolidation of the cannabis industry is desirable because it increases their access to high-quality cannabis at more affordable prices:

> I think [corporation have impacted the industry] positively. . . . . It's an incredibly wealth-intensive industry and you see these "grows," they just cost a fortune . . . and then all the taxes you have to pay and the testing and then you have to buy the testing machines. Without [corporations] I think it just would be so much slower to get going if you want to have a really robust regulated industry, which is what I think also is what you want to have.

The vast majority of people will experience legal cannabis this way. When they walk into a dispensary they will be greeted by a clean, well-lit facility, with a helpful "bud tender" to guide them through an impressive list of affordable cannabis products. Most will probably walk away from the experience satisfied, without worrying too much about the government policies and market forces that helped create it.

But many long-standing members of the cannabis community who tried to make the transition to the legal market are losing their livelihoods as a result of these changes. Catherine told me that she thought this was too high a cost to pay for cheap weed. "A lot of . . . [people] took so much risk to be able to cultivate a little bit of cannabis . . . for so many years. . . . And I think that if those folks who have been cultivating for ten, twenty years can't continue to cultivate then I personally don't consider legalization a success." This loss of livelihood is devastating for these individuals, many of whom have spent decades working in the cannabis trade. They lack the legitimate work experience necessary to get jobs in other industries and will struggle to make ends meet without their cannabis income.

As these longstanding members of the cannabis community leave, the industry becomes dominated by people who had little to no prior relationship with the cannabis plant. This has begun to change the entire culture around cannabis. Kimberly explained:

> What I saw happening [in my state] is people getting into the industry that didn't really care about cannabis. They cared about making money. . . . And so, the approach to what's being produced is very different. . . . The culture of cannabis historically has been [about] . . . being a disrupter . . . of the systems that are in place that benefit a few but not the many. The opportunity that we have with cannabis legalization is to continue to do some disruption around those systems. . . . Can we not start a new way of looking at how we structure our businesses where we're environmentally conscious, where we care about paying our workers a decent wage, we care about the planet and people over profits, right? Unfortunately, without being tapped into that initial culture of why we are here, that sort of disrupter culture, it's going [away].

Kenneth's small cannabis business embodied the outsider politics of the original cannabis community. Yet, he found that most of the cannabis industry was uninterested in, or even hostile to, the values that he and his business partner were trying to advance. He told me:

> Another layer to this is what it has been like for us to be queer people . . . and to be overtly antiracist people inside of an industry that is wildly white, and that is mostly straight, and that is mostly top-heavy in terms of cis, white

men. What is it like for us as queer people to go into a retail location and try to tell the story that we are telling, which is queering the planet, queering the industry, queering the plant? Obviously we don't use that word, because most retail buyers would be like, "What the fuck are you talking about?" How do we tell that story while also holding true to our ethics, which is we're not selling you schwag weed right now. This is really, really sacred stuff. The body is sacred and the planet is sacred. It's been interesting for us to navigate those waters.

The cannabis community has historically been one of the few places where people like Kenneth could go to find allies. As corporations begin to take over the industry, those once-welcoming spaces are beginning to disappear.

Left Behind: Operating in the Illicit Cannabis Space Post-Legalization

> Cannabis existed parallel to all other corporations in America. . . . It already had its own system that was very successful. . . . And then . . . corporate cannabis comes in, right, and it's big money, and guys from Yale with MBAs, and . . . they have the know-how because business is business. . . . But then what happens to those people who since 1938 have been growing in the hills, have been feeding their families?
> —Guy (cannabis activist)

Much has been reported about the creative potential of legal cannabis. It is estimated that this new industry could generate hundreds of billions of dollars for the US economy (McVey 2020) and create hundreds of thousands of jobs in both "plant touching" and ancillary businesses (Barcott, Whitney, and Bailey 2021). But there is a destructive side to legal cannabis as well. This "new" cannabis industry has not been created on a tabula rasa. Instead, it is being constructed on the foundation of an already existing illicit and quasi-legal medical industry. Ideally, those operating in the illicit or medical cannabis space would be able to transition to the legal market. But as we have seen, it is exceedingly difficult for them to do so successfully. As such, legalizing cannabis does not just mean creating new opportunities, it is also means destroying the more informal economic opportunities that had existed in the illicit and medial cannabis spaces previously. What happens to the members of the cannabis community that legalization has left behind?

Illicit Cannabis Is an Economic Lifeline for Many

People operating in the illicit cannabis space are often stereotyped as violent criminals or gang members (see, for example, Drug Enforcement Agency 2020b, 54), but studies of the illicit cannabis industry have found that the vast majority of the people working in it have no history of violence, and no known ties to organized crime (Weisheit 1992; Schlosser 2003, 11–74). One of the reasons that illicit cannabis is so attractive to many, is that the barriers to entry are extremely low. Unlike cocaine or heroin, which must be grown in tropical climates, or synthetics, which must be created in a laboratory using expensive equipment, cannabis can be grown domestically with relative ease. And, unlike with legitimate businesses, one does not need to know how to construct a business plan, hire employees, or pay taxes to sell cannabis on the illicit market. As a result, cannabis often serves as an informal means of economic support for people who have found it difficult to earn a living in the legitimate economy.

People struggle to find work in the legitimate economy for a variety of reasons. They may have a criminal record or lack access to the necessary capital. They may also struggle to be taken seriously in a professional space because they have visible tattoos or are unable to adopt a more professional communication style, often referred to as "code switching" (McCluney et al. 2019). The illicit cannabis trade has none of these requirements, making it a much more accessible, and in many ways, more equitable economic system. Carl shared with me how illicit cannabis has historically acted as a refuge for people like this:

> What struck me was the amount of folks that were involved at the ownership level in this kind of market, that were people who were down and out. A lot of folks who were dealing with the fallout of the financial crisis, but also a lot of folks who've never really been able to participate in the formal economy for a lot of other reasons. . . . They were trimmers, they were small-time dealers,

they were small-time growers. They could bring their tiny little crops to the dispensary and it would get sold. It struck me as a particularly democratic economy.

For others, illicit cannabis acts as supplemental income. They may have a legitimate job, but maybe it does not pay well enough for them to live a comfortable middle-class lifestyle. So they sell a little cannabis to get ahead. Catherine explains:

> It used to be, before legalization, that marijuana sales were this economic equalizer. So, folks who, for whatever reason, couldn't make enough money working their day job to make ends meet would grow some marijuana on the side. And so, a lot of the guys that I know, they were carpenters full time, or construction workers full time, regular blue-collar jobs, and then on the side they'd grow some marijuana in their basement or their garage and that helped them pay off property. That helped them put food on the table for their kids and pay for Christmas and travel and that sort of thing.

The earning power of the average American family has remained stagnant since the 1970s, as wages have barely kept up with inflation. Blue-collar workers have been particularly hard hit by these trends, with studies indicating that their real wages have actually declined over this time period (Congressional Research Service 2020). Given that, it is unsurprising that many working-class people have turned to cannabis to help make ends meet.

The economic opportunities that the illicit cannabis industry provides are especially important for people of color, who often have more difficulty succeeding in the legitimate economy, because they must contend with racial discrimination. Guy, a Black cannabis activist in Washington, explained to me how informal cannabis markets were used by his community to offset the economic costs of racism:

> [I grew up] in a blue-collar community that used cannabis as a means to sustain their family livelihood when work got bad, because they were all construction workers. . . . Black construction workers are usually the last one hired and the first one fired, so these men were laid off quite often. And then, so to combat that being laid off all the time . . . they would substitute that loss income working with the cannabis trade. . . . I grew up in a community of cannabis growers, sellers, trimmers, the whole everything. And I watched cannabis from day one sustain communities. It kept alcoholism off of my street, it kept drug addiction off my street, it kept [away] violence, divorce.

The illicit drug trade is often thought of as having had a destabilizing effect on Black and brown communities. Here, Guy turns this argument on its head, pointing out that in many ways the illicit cannabis industry actually helps to stabilize these communities by providing badly needed economic resources.

Of course, operating in the illicit cannabis industry comes with considerable costs as well. Besides the obvious risks of legal reprisal, experience in the illicit industry also acts as a negative credential for potential employers in the legitimate economy. Since this activity is highly stigmatized, any experience that is gained operating in this environment is at best severely discounted, and at worst counterproductive to getting a legitimate job. This makes it even harder for these people to transition to the legitimate economy, should they need to do so. This has left many people without a clear plan for what they are going to do when the illicit cannabis trade disappears. Catherine told me:

> What happens when you take away income opportunities for this group of people? What options are available to them? And I can say that I've had [illicit cannabis] farmers tell me that they needed to get an off-farm job because the price of pot has fallen, and they're struggling to find an off-farm job because their choices are to put their marijuana cultivation business on their resume, or to have a blank on their resume. And neither of those . . . are ideal. . . . What are these guys who've been growing for ten, twenty years, what are they going to go do next?

The impact of this loss of revenue is enormous, and it is felt not just by those individuals who are participating in the illicit industry directly but also by the entire community that they support. Eric, a Black cannabis activist in Illinois, told me:

> With the legalization of cannabis, you took a billion dollars off the street. Illegal, legal, or whatever. I don't care what industry that is. If you pull a billion dollars out of it, it's going to have a negative effect on the people that's in that industry. . . . Say you have a felony, you come home. You can't get housing, you can't get food stamps, and you have no education. Cannabis became a business to a lot of people to feed their families. And now that money isn't there anymore.

A lot of the people working in the illicit cannabis industry have spent their entire lives doing so. Their families depend on cannabis dollars, and in

many cases they have no other trade to fall back on should those opportunities disappear.

For-Profit Industry Harms Medical Cannabis Patients and Providers

For some, the choice to continue operating in the illicit cannabis space
after legalization has less to do with money and more to do with values.
One of the aspects of cannabis legalization that has received little coverage
from the media is the impact that it has had on the medical cannabis community. In theory, legalizing cannabis for adult use should have no impact
on medical cannabis patients, who can continue to purchase cannabis on
the legal market as they did before. In reality, however, legal cannabis
has been a disaster for the medical cannabis community. Many medical
cannabis activists have spent decades advocating for cannabis reform, not
because they wanted to make a profit but because they believed strongly
in the medicinal power of the plant. Indeed, the desire to make a profit
and the desire to unlock the medical potential of cannabis are often at
odds with one another. As such, many of the corporations who supported
medical cannabis initially lost interest once the more lucrative adult-use
cannabis industry emerged. This has left many medical cannabis patients
and activists feeling angry and betrayed. Henry, for example, told me,

> We've been screwed by the wealthy, corporate interests who have
> no interest in medical cannabis. When you go to these cannabis
> conferences, they give practically no shrift . . . to medical issues.
> And all it's about is how much fucking money they can make.
> Excuse my language. But that's all they fucking care about, is
> how much money they can make.

One way in which the desire for profit clashes with the interests of
medical cannabis patients is with the development of different strains of
the cannabis plant. Certain strains of cannabis have been shown to be
particularly helpful for medical cannabis patients, but they tend to be
low-yielding varieties, which means most big cannabis corporations are
not interested in selling them. Catherine explained:

I think that there's a lot of really wonderful cannabis strains and cultivars that are held by some of the small operators because there are some strains that are really wonderful and really effective, but they aren't the highest yielders. And so, you won't see the big guys cultivating theses strains because it's only about numbers for them, right? If they're after the highest yield, shortest flower time, and whatever is going to maximize their profits.

As a result, some of the strains that have been painstakingly developed by medical cannabis providers for their medicinal qualities are at risk of being lost as a result of cannabis legalization. Jennifer, a medical cannabis provider who developed a number of cannabis strains with powerful medicinal qualities, told me, "We put hundreds of thousands of dollars over time into the building that we were breeding the strains . . . not only the rent, but a big electric bill, and the testing of every strain. . . . We spent all that money, and developed what we have developed, and I don't have anybody that wants it, or will allow me to take it further."

Another issue is that legal cannabis is often too expensive for medical patients to afford. In some states medical cannabis patients are exempt from paying state taxes on cannabis, allowing them to purchase products at a slightly discounted rate. But even these discounted rates are still too high for many medical cannabis patients, and because the federal government has deemed cannabis to be without medical value, it is not covered by medical insurance plans. Prior to adult-use legalization, many medical cannabis providers in states like Oregon, California, or Washington, where the medical cannabis industry was spottily regulated (at best), compensated for this by providing cannabis to medical patients in need at sharply discounted rates, or even giving it away for free. This practice was prohibited after these states legalized cannabis for adult use.

This puts medical cannabis providers in a difficult position. Many feel like they are being forced to choose between serving patients in need or following the legal regulations established by their state. Harriet, a long-time cannabis activist and medical cannabis provider, described her dilemma to me this way:

Legalization puts me in the situation where the government can tell me that I can't give purely tested cannabis to children whose parents are being asked to spend the last dime out of their pocketbooks making decisions about whether "I'm going to feed my kids or take my other kids to treatment this week." You know? It's part of this corrupt medical system that we've got that somehow suggests that all of your assets should be drained because you have the bad luck of getting sick.

Harriet is not alone. Many of the medical cannabis providers that I talked with for this study shared their difficulty transition from a medical cannabis space, which placed the well-being of patients first, to an adult-use marketplace, which values profits above all else. Jennifer, for example, told me, "Which of the people that I give medicine to because they don't have money am I going to say 'I'm sorry, I can't do this for you anymore'? It's crazy that they put us in this position, but nobody cares. Nobody cares."

Medical providers like Jennifer and Harriet, who have continued to operate in the illicit market post-legalization, do so at considerable risk to their own well-being. This causes an understandable amount of stress and anxiety. Jennifer told me that she would like to transition to the legal marketplace but finds the barriers to entry to be too steep. According to her:

> I have never had the money, personally, to be able to [transition to the legal market] because our collective, basically, every time we could lower the prices, we did, because that's what we were supposed to do. . . . We were just trying to help people, and now we got kicked to the curb without any sort of a gold medal for any of the work we've done. . . . I'm left in a not-legal environment where I have recently been extorted, and I've had police come to my door. I want to be protected.

Jennifer has chosen to remain in the illicit market, where she continues to serve the needs of her patients. But doing so puts her in an incredibly vulnerable position, and she is unsure how long she can carry on.

Other medical providers remained defiant, however. Harriet has no desire to ever enter the legal cannabis space. For her, serving medical cannabis patients is an act of civil disobedience—one that she would be proud to martyr herself for, if necessary. She told me:

> I am unafraid of power at this point. . . . I shout from stages everywhere, "if you know any ill or terminally ill children, or veterans, send them to me. I will treat them." . . . I used to be very frightened about being arrested. . . . I'm completely unafraid now. Because I know that there are so many people who have observed me and the way that I act and the way that I work with cannabis, they're going to be there on the courthouse steps. I'm happy to two-step around the courtroom with anyone. I'm just old enough. My attorneys tell

me they'd probably keep me out of jail for the rest of my natural life. Let's go. Let's have a talk about freedom. Because cannabis doesn't need regulation.

Harriet may not be worried about being arrested, but she is an eloquent defendant with the resources to mount a powerful legal defense. Since she is also as an older white woman, it is also likely that she would be viewed with some sympathy by a jury, lessening her chances of receiving a harsh prison sentence. Many others who continue to operate in the illicit cannabis space after legalization are not so fortunate.

Struggling to Compete with Legal Cannabis

What happens to the people who were operating in the illicit cannabis industry prior to legalization when they cannot transition to the legal marketplace? A lot depends on how the state has structured its legal cannabis regulations. In states like Oregon or Washington, where barriers to entry have been relatively low, increased competition has driven the price of legal cannabis down. This may be good news for cannabis consumers, but it makes things difficult for those trying to operate in the illicit cannabis space. As a result, a good number of them end up leaving the industry altogether. Jody told me:

> I probably knew fifty people that grew cannabis during the medical days. . . . Not one of those people are still growing. Most of them are blowing glass, actually. Or they tried to get a job in the legal market but nobody could pay what they were worth. . . . We have lost so many good people, and we've lost so many good growers and have lost so many good [plant] genetics.

In other states, however, the illicit cannabis industry has proven more resilient. In states like Illinois, where regulations are tight and taxes are high, the cost of legal cannabis can be as much as double what it typically sells for on the illicit market. As a result, the state's illicit cannabis industry is thriving (Schuba 2021b).

Another reason for the persistence of the illicit market is that many of the people operating in that space feel like they have no other options. Growing and selling cannabis is sometimes the only thing they know how to do that can generate a living wage. The choice is between going hungry and being unable to pay one's bills, or risking jail time. It is not a particularly difficult decision. Todd, who operates an illicit cannabis dispensary in California, told me:

> These are good people that are just trying to earn a living. And they have no pathway to . . . get their license. So, they're all just saying, "Hey, screw it. I got to put dinner on the table." That's kind of where that's at with the illegal market. . . . In California especially, we been doing this for generations. . . . So, we got this. That's the feeling with everybody, is that, "Hey, we got this." Our [customers] have been with us for ten years now. . . . And they love exactly what I'm doing. They don't care whether I'm legal or not.

This is not false bravado. California has been trying to crush the illicit cannabis industry by force in places like the Emerald Triangle for more than half a century, with little to show for its efforts.

Unless the price of legal cannabis comes down, the state is unlikely to have any more success prosecuting the illicit industry now, than it had before cannabis was legalized. Julie explains:

> I think [the state has] doubled the amount of money they're spending on enforcement. . . . [But] these people have been underground for years. . . . You're not gonna find a man who's been growing for thirty or forty years and has sent his kids to college, you're not gonna convince him that he's gotta quit what he's doing and go find a regular job where they're gonna pay him eleven bucks an hour.

There is precedent for the continued operation of an illicit industry for a legal substance, especially if the state artificially inflates prices through taxation. Tobacco is legal in all fifty states, yet that has not stopped a thriving illicit market for cigarettes, often sold individually as "loosies," from developing in many US cities (Smith et al. 2007). Of course, participating in this illicit economy comes with risk of arrest, or even death at the hands of law enforcement officials—as the tragic case of Eric Garner illustrates (Baker, Goodman, and Mueller 2015).

It may be difficult for the state to ever completely eradicate the illicit industry by force, but economic pressure from the legal cannabis industry may do the job for them. As the legal cannabis market matures, and prices become more competitive, it is likely that most cannabis consumers will eventually migrate to the legal market (Donnan et al. 2022). Another factor helping to support the illicit cannabis industry currently is that cannabis is still prohibited by federal law. This means that it is illegal for people who grow cannabis for the legal market in one state to sell it in another, even if that state has also legalized cannabis. As a result, those with surplus cannabis crops in states like California, Oregon, or Michigan have no choice but to unload their excess crop on the illicit market. Much of it ends up traveling across state lines (Fertig 2019). But it seems inevitable that those federal prohibitions will someday be lifted, and when they are, it is likely to put even more market pressure on the illicit cannabis industry. Jody told me:

> That illicit market, it's not a long-term solution. . . . It's really short sighted, right? If you look at alcohol prohibition, you probably got ten years of bathtub gin that you can continue to sell. But after that, you're done. . . . There is zero chance I would be involved in those [illicit] markets at this point in time. Now, I don't have any problem with other people [doing it]. . . . But for us and from a long-term strategy standpoint, there's zero chance I can be involved in any of that.

The state has spent decades unsuccessfully trying to eradicate cannabis through a highly punitive War on Drugs. It is perhaps a little ironic that legalizing cannabis nationwide may be the thing that ultimately results in the eradication of the illicit cannabis industry.

FOUR

Sustaining a Movement

Mobilizing for Cannabis Reform After Legalization

The media, and even many members of the cannabis community, often talk about cannabis legalization as if it represents the ultimate victory for the cannabis reform movement. Yet, from the perspective of many activists, legalization is just one step in an ongoing struggle for a more humane and socially responsible approach to cannabis. They see cannabis reform as a mechanism for addressing a long list of social justice causes, such as reforming our criminal justice system, promoting racial and economic equality, or providing better access to affordable healthcare. This project began long before legalizing cannabis was a realistic possibility and will continue long after it has been accomplished. This complicates simplistic depictions of cannabis reform as a movement with one goal and one goal only—"legalize it!"

What comes next for the cannabis reform movement? How do activists who are operating in legal cannabis states sustain momentum after achieving a long-sought victory? And what new tactics must they use to succeed in a post legalization environment? Answering these questions will help illuminate some of the challenges facing activists who continue to fight for social change in the aftermath a major victory. Social scientists have long used the "political process model" to explain the rise and fall of social movements. This model focuses primarily on how social movements respond to external "opportunity structures" (McAdam 1999). According to this model, movements succeed by effectively organizing and framing their cause so they are able to capitalize on different windows of opportunity. They falter when they are ill prepared to capitalize on those opportunities, or when those windows of opportunity close (Meyer 2004). Since these opportunities are ephemeral, even successful movements have distinct "life cycles," featuring a gradual rise, leading to the accomplishment of a key breakthrough, followed by an inevitable decline, as the opportunity structure changes (Tarrow 2011). These same dynamics have shaped the cannabis reform movement. This chapter documents how cannabis activists navigate the inevitable post legalization decline. Cannabis reform activists working in legal cannabis states report a noticeable drop in enthusiasm of late as they struggle to raise capital, build solidarity, and mobilize supporters without a highly salient cause like legalization to rally behind.

Cannabis legalization also has the effect of "expanding the scope of the contagion" of the conflict over cannabis reform (Schattschneider 1960). Legalization changes the nature of the debate over cannabis from a relatively simple conflict between cannabis reform activists on one side, and law enforcement officials and concerned parent groups on the other, into a complicated dispute involving a host of different actors. It creates new stakeholders such as corporations, security companies, laboratory technicians, and commercial property owners, who have very different ideas about what cannabis reform should look like. It also has the effect of shifting the terrain of this debate from one-off political campaigns, which lend themselves well to grassroots organizing, to the constant grind of legislative rulemaking, which does not. This further complicates the efforts of activists, requiring them to adjust their tactics and learn new strategies.

These challenges suggest that reforming the laws and regulations governing legal cannabis may be even harder than legalizing cannabis was in the first place. As E. E. Schattschneider warned in *Semisovereign People*, "so great is the change in the nature of any conflict likely to be as a consequence of the widening involvement of people in it that the original participants are apt to lose control of the conflict altogether" (1960, 3). Indeed, shifting the debate over cannabis reform to a regulatory environment places activists at a disadvantage relative to deep-pocketed business interests who use their considerable resources to hire lobbyists and influence the legislative process. This highlights the importance of drafting robust legalization bills, which put progressive values at the forefront, rather than accepting flawed cannabis legislation in the hopes of reforming it later.

Herding Cats: The Struggle to Mobilize a Diverse Coalition of Cannabis Activists

> When we talk about "there's a movement," first of all, what do we even mean? . . . To think that this is some sort of monolithic movement, or to think that there is some hierarchy, where individuals at the top send out their talking points. . . . We're not that kind of a movement. . . . It's much like herding cats.
> —Sean (cannabis activist)

Social movements are often conceptualized as temporally bound, monolithic entities, dedicated to a clear set of agreed-upon principles. The reality is more complicated. Social movements are not fixed things, rather they are constantly evolving projects, "never formed, but always forming" (Mayo-Adams 2020, 1). This is certainly the case for cannabis reform. Like all movements, it is made up of a coalition of activists from a range of different organizations, all with their own unique histories, perspectives, and agendas. These groups may agree to work together for a time, when their interests align, but these alliances are tenuous and can easily fracture as the situation changes, such as in the aftermath of a major breakthrough. Cannabis legalization has often served as a way to unify cannabis reform activists, but once this goal has been achieved, the fractures within this movement become more difficult to address.

Toward a More Inclusive Cannabis Reform Movement

The term "cannabis community," which I have been using throughout this book, is a convenient shorthand, but it might give the impression that this group is more cohesive than it really is. People are attracted to cannabis reform for a variety of different, often deeply personal, reasons. Some are medical cannabis patients, others work in the cannabis industry, and still others see cannabis as a vehicle for promoting social justice causes like racial or gender equity. These activists also come from different racial, class, gender, and ideological backgrounds. These different identities intersect to shape how they view the cause of cannabis reform. Activists may share a common desire to reform our cannabis laws, but they often have very different ideas about what that reform should look like.

The cannabis reform movement has not always done a great job of making sure that all of these different perspectives are well represented. The community of people who enjoy cannabis has always been pretty diverse, but until recently cannabis activists, especially those in leadership positions at influential national organizations like NORML, MPP, and DPA, were primarily white men. This has created a distinct generational divide within the cannabis reform movement today. Most of the "old guard" first got involved with this movement during the 1970s–1990s. They are almost all white and disproportionately male. Since these activists have been involved in this movement for so long, they make up a disproportionate share of the movement's leadership base. This gives them more power to decide how scarce resources are allocated, and more opportunity to shape the movement's national agenda.

The cannabis reform movement has seen an influx of young activists of late. This younger generation of activists is far more diverse with respect to race and gender than those who came before them. This has caused tension within the movement. Many activists of color feel that leadership does not really understand their perspective and does not know how to advocate for cannabis reform in a way that best suits their community. Sara told me:

> When we look at the faces of the leading people in the [cannabis] advocacy community, not just politicians, but the people on the ground, grassroots, they're overwhelmingly white and most of them are men. Those are not the people that have been criminalized, right? I'd love to see more African Americans get involved. . . . Sometimes the allies can be a little bit blinded. . . . I think we should have more leaders and more people face forward in the movement who can really speak . . . of their own experience.

Communities of color suffered the greatest harms from cannabis prohibition, yet the cannabis reform movement has, until very recently, given scant attention to issues of race. This is in part because the leadership of the cannabis reform movement has been overwhelmingly white.

Younger cannabis activists also grew up in a time in which cannabis was more culturally acceptable. As a result, they tend to have goals for cannabis reform that are more ambitious than their more seasoned colleagues. One young activist told me:

> The old guard at [my organization], rightfully so, felt like they had accomplished what they had been fighting for, legalization. Whereas a bunch of the new recruits . . . were significantly younger than the guys who've been on the board since the '70s. A lot of us have taken on the new role because we realized that even though legalization was a huge step in the correct direction, there's also some unintended consequences that have happened, and there's tons of advocacy work that still needs to be done.

Yet, because these activists are new to the movement, few have been able to rise to positions of leadership, giving them less influence over the direction of cannabis reform.

Many of the young cannabis activists who spoke with me for this study felt frustrated by their lack of power within the movement. They reported feeling ignored by leadership and lacking efficacy. Sara told me, with thinly veiled contempt:

> The old guard is overwhelmingly white, overwhelmingly male, which makes them even more myopic than most of the other advocates, especially the younger ones. . . . I think that older people tend to believe that they are the smartest people in the room. . . . [But] either you do the work or get out of the way. . . . Because we don't have time for this. People are still going to jail. People are still living with these federal consequences. People are still losing their fathers and mothers to the criminal justice system. . . . People's feelings are going to get hurt because people want to feel important [but] . . . forgive me if I don't want to coddle . . . a sixty-year-old man who wants to hold on to this until you die. I don't really care about that. . . . If you are not going to do the work, get out of the way.

For activists like Sara, these generational divides are less about substantive differences, and more about the old guard's desire to preserve their status and power. If the cannabis reform movement is going to remain relevant it will need to figure out how to better incorporate the perspectives of younger activists like her, but doing so may require working on an individual level to soothe egos and manage interpersonal conflicts.

The more senior activists that I talked with for this study were ambivalent about the generational power struggle within the cannabis reform movement. Some criticized younger activists for being naïve and thought that they were too quick to dismiss the accomplishments of previous generations. Kimberly, for example, told me, "The younger generation, honestly, have no idea that they're benefiting from the work of generations of people, and it didn't come easy, and there are people still in prison. . . . There's a whole history of why we got here in the first place that is being overlooked, in some ways kind of looked down at." Others saw the naïveté of younger activists as an asset to the movement. Tamara, a longtime cannabis activist who often works closely with students, told me:

> There is no social justice movement or civil rights event of the last, at least, sixty or seventy years but perhaps longer, that has succeeded in the US, and perhaps worldwide, without an informed, empowered, and supported student or youth contingent. And so, there's not really any reason to think that the drug policy or marijuana policy reform even would be any different. . . . Any movement needs young people, and the value the young people bring to a movement in terms of having a vision that's broader than, or more far-reaching than those of us with fully developed frontal lobes are able to muster is really important. And so, I'm always looking to our members and other youth activists in this movement to sort of tell me what's next, tell me what we need to be working on. Because they have that further vision, and I'm ready for them to be in charge in a lot of ways.

As Tamara suggests, young activists have often brought fresh perspectives to social movements, challenging the entrenched views of more seasoned activists, and pushing them in a more radical direction.

Cannabis Legalization and Solidarity

The fact that the cannabis reform movement must contend with internal divisions is not surprising. All successful social movements must figure out a way to build solidarity among the disparate elements of their community. To do this, movements work to get their members to find common ground around shared policy goals, form coalitions with sympathetic organizations, and develop unity slogans to rally around (Tarrow 2011, 119–56). Despite their racial, class, and gender differences, cannabis activists all typically do have one thing in common—a shared love of the cannabis plant itself. This often serves as a bridge, helping to bring together people who would otherwise have very little in common. Jeffrey told me:

> The cannabis plant, it's such an effective medium to bring people [together]. . . . We can connect all these different things together through cannabis, and . . . just open up doors for conversations that probably never would have happened without that vehicle. . . . There's just so much that can be shared, and it really is a special thing, and so I would definitely say the coalition has benefited from cannabis being a vehicle like that to open minds and to open doors.

Cannabis activists may have a shared love of cannabis but, as we have seen, that does not necessarily mean they share the same opinions about how best to reform their nation's drug laws.

One thing that most cannabis activists have tended to agree on, however, is that cannabis should be legalized. Indeed, legalization has often been used as a common goal to rally the disparate elements of the cannabis reform movement. But just because these activists support legalization in theory does not mean that they support the specific cannabis legalization bills that have been put before voters. Many people in the cannabis community had to be convinced that supporting these statutes was in their best interest. Perhaps no group has been more skeptical of legalization than medical cannabis patients and providers. Medical cannabis is currently permitted in thirty-eight states, so most medical cannabis patients already enjoy easy access to retail cannabis.[1] As such, many reason that they have much to lose from legalization, and little to gain.

Convincing these skeptical elements of the cannabis community to support legalization efforts became a major focus of legalization campaigns. Stephanie, a cannabis activist who worked on the legalization campaign in Washington, told me:

> There was a very organized patient group in Washington that they were protected under the existing kind of medical laws and they liked the rather somewhat spottily unregulated market. . . . So, the patient community was

existing within that gap, and some of the most radical members really opposed all legalization, because they said it would be the end of medical.

Other medical cannabis activists expressed concerns that legalizing cannabis would cause prices to increase, making it difficult for some patients to afford their medicine. Wanda, for example, told me, "I don't think patients should be paying a tax to support the success of the recreational system . . . we were the bulk of the market, so [the state said] 'if we do this tax, and we don't allow the patients to pay it, we let them out of it, then we don't have the money to keep us afloat.' We were cash cows."

Yet, despite these concerns most, though certainly not all, medical cannabis patients and providers did ultimately agree to work together to support these legalization efforts because they felt that doing so was in the best interest of the movement overall. It took some convincing, but Stephanie told me that she was able to get most of the people she talked with from the medical cannabis community to support cannabis legalization in her state. According to her, "When people [in the medical cannabis community] would say, 'Oh my God, the sky is going to fall, this is going to change medical . . .' I would often respond with 'this legalization is not perfect. The legislation is incremental, but you cannot underestimate the damage this does to the wall of federal prohibition if we legalize.' And so, with that driving force we just firmly were in favor." Beulah, a medical cannabis patient and activist in California, spoke for many when she told me:

> I was worried how [legalization] was going to affect medical marijuana . . . but I knew that overall, it was going to be a good thing for the majority of the state, for a majority of cannabis consumers, and that it was going to move us in the right direction. I knew that if it failed it would be detrimental not just for the cannabis community in general, but the whole country, you know? . . . I was really glad that it [passed].

Now that cannabis has been legalized in several states, these shared bonds have begun to fray. Many activists like Beulah, who held their nose and voted for legalization, now have serious regrets. Harriet, for example, lamented that legalization had paved the way for a corporate takeover of cannabis, something that she feared would destroy the medical cannabis community. She told me:

> We're mad. We had a vision of the way that it should be. . . . We had an operating medical system. . . . And it was just snagged away from us. . . . . We misarticulated what it was we were looking for. We were actually asking for freedom in cannabis but in the persecution and prosecution of our community members, we made a shorthand which said legalization, which was merely the framework to allow those who misunderstand the plant to take control.

Many medical cannabis patients and providers supported legalization because, they were tired of the unpredictable way in which medical cannabis laws were enforced. They shared horror stories about the federal government raiding medical cannabis providers who were openly growing cannabis in full compliance with state law. Legalization seemed like a way to prevent this from happening, by giving medial cannabis patients and providers more protection from law enforcement. But, as Harriet suggests, in their desire to prevent more arrests they passed laws that merely exchanged one form of control for another, more insidious one.

Efforts are being made to address these issues, and many activists are optimistic that with time, they will be able to amend these laws to address at least some of these concerns. But reforming cannabis laws so that they better serve the interests of medical cannabis patients would almost certainly mean fewer profits for the corporations who backed legalization in the first place, and less tax revenue for the state. This has made it very difficult for medical cannabis activists to reform cannabis laws post-legalization. Wanda told me:

> Those of us who didn't get with the program were demonized because we were "letting the perfect be the enemy of the good" …They all told me "don't let the perfect be the enemy of the good. Pass it now and fix it later." And it's like okay, so we did. And who has fixed it? We don't have home grows, the five nanogram hasn't been fixed, patients lost access to their medicine, the tax hasn't been fixed.

Many in the medical cannabis community feel used. For them, legalization feels less like the culmination of decades of hard work, and more like a hostile takeover. In a post-legalization environment, the conversation has shifted away from embracing the medical potential of cannabis, and more toward maximizing profits. This has left the cannabis community even more fractured than they were before cannabis was legalized.

Maintaining Enthusiasm for Reform Post-Legalization

In addition to helping bring together disparate elements of the cannabis community, the fight to legalize cannabis also helped energize and excite people, allowing activists to build a broader coalition and more effectively mobilize supporters. But once legalization has been achieved, many of these new activists tend to fall away. Most of the people that I talked with for this study reported a noticeable drop in enthusiasm for cannabis reform after legalization. Terry told me, "It's extremely difficult to get people to believe that there's still danger in Michigan when it comes to cannabis use. And without the perception of danger, there is very little activism to be had. It is extremely difficult for organizations that I represent . . . to recruit members at this point because there's a great perception that job done, everybody go home." Abel, an activist in California, made a similar observation, "It's hard to undo a lot of this bad stuff that's been done, to tell you the truth. . . . We've certainly lost a lot of interest here in California from users since Prop 64. Everybody figures well, it's legal now . . . there's a lot of indifference or whatever now that it's been legalized."

One sign that the grassroots enthusiasm for cannabis reform may be on the wane is the declining attendance at annual cannabis rallies like Hash Bash in Ann Arbor, Michigan, the Boston Freedom Rally, or Hemp Fest in Seattle. These annual events are part political protest, part neighborhood block party. They have a carnival atmosphere, typically featuring speeches from cannabis activists and celebrities, live music, food, and plenty of cannabis merchandise. They also serve as crucial opportunities for cannabis activists from around the country to meet up, share ideas, and plan for the future. Wanda explained:

[Hemp Fest] started in '91, so seven years before there was a medical program in Washington. . . . It was an act of civil disobedience, that was the whole point, was we are going to get together, 50 strong, 500 strong, 5,000 strong growing every year, and we're going to smoke pot in the park and there's nothing they're going to do because they can't take all 50, or 500, or 5,000 of us. . . . Probably more than anything else, it unites us activists from around the country and we all reconnect every year, and we're able to exchange stories about what happened in our area . . . we can exchange ideas and connect with each other and support each other through that.

At its peak, Hemp Fest would draw more than 250,000 people over the course of a single weekend. These days, the festival is lucky to attract 100,000. Wanda told me:

> It's legalization that's going to be the death now of Hemp Fest. Because the people don't feel they need to come anymore, because it's legal so we don't need to protest. . . . Every year the media asks me, "Why is Hemp Fest still relevant?" . . . and then I have to say, "Because people still can't get organ transplants if they use cannabis, people still have their kids taken if they use cannabis. People are denied student loans for cannabis, people are losing their housing over cannabis. All of these reasons it's still relevant." So as long as we have these civil rights battles and more, as long as patients can't afford access to their medicine, I'm going to be there and Hemp Fest is going to be there helping educate people.

The decline of Hemp Fest may seem like a trivial matter when compared to more weighty issues like criminal justice reform or building an equitable cannabis industry. If events like this continue to wane in popularity, however, members of the cannabis community will have lost not only a chance to get together and have a good time, but also a valuable opportunity to recruit new activists.

In an effort to compensate for the decline in grassroots enthusiasm for cannabis reform, many activists have argued for a tactical shift away from volunteer grassroots organizing, toward a more elite driven strategy, which is reliant on a smaller group of paid professional lobbyists. But this approach is made difficult by the fact national cannabis activist organizations typically stop investing in legal cannabis states post-legalization. Jeffrey, an activist in Illinois, told me:

> It's not just enough to legalize, you have to see it through. . . . There was a lot of speeches made on the House and Senate floor, there was a lot of speeches the governor made that we're going to do this, we're going to do that, it's going to be great. And then we legalized it, everybody packed up and went home. . . . There's a couple of [national cannabis] organizations . . . that I've had some issues with, because they came in . . . with paid lobbyists and paid professionals to get [legalization] done, and then walk away. . . . I [take] issue with folks who pack up their bags as soon as [legalization is] over, because it's literally just the beginning.

Effectively implementing cannabis legalization, so that it functions as intended, is a much harder task than getting the state to agree to legalize cannabis in the first place. It will require a considerable financial investment to be successful. This puts social justice–oriented advocacy groups, who tend to operate on a shoestring budget, at a distinct disadvantage as compared to their more well-financed peers in the business sector.

Expanding the Scope of the Contagion: The Regulatory Battle for Cannabis Reform

> A lot of people have this facile idea that everything is fine now that we legalized it. As I said, the devil's in the details of regulation and boy are there a lot of details.
> —Henry (cannabis activist)

Cannabis legalization represents a transition point for the cannabis reform movement. Having successfully convinced lawmakers to support the idea of legalization, these activists must now begin the more practical job of putting in place rules and regulations that translate this desire into reality. This process of regulatory rulemaking is, in many ways, even more important than the battle over whether or not to legalize cannabis in the first place. As one activist told me, "Really where the important stuff is happening is at that less glamorous, day to day policymaking that occurs at the regulatory bodies." Yet, it receives very little attention from the media or the general public. The policymaking process is often compared unfavorably to sausage making. For many Americans regulatory rulemaking seems arcane, tedious, and unsavory. As a result, most know very little about how their regulatory sausage is made—and they like it that way. This dynamic poses a problem for the cannabis reform movement, which has typically relied on the enthusiasm of its grassroots volunteer base to pressure legislative officials to act.

Reluctant Radicals: From Cannabis Business Owner to Cannabis Activist

The general public may not have much interest in shaping the regulatory rules governing the cannabis industry, but those working in this industry certainly do. For those on the receiving end of these new rules and regulations, many of whom had never participated in social movement activism before, mobilizing for cannabis reform has become a matter of survival. Catherine and her husband became active in the fight for cannabis reform after being confronted with a number of unexpected regulatory rule changes that would have devastate their small cannabis farm before it even got started. She told me that "I sort of came to realize that in order for regular small businesses to be able to participate in this industry we were going to have to really engage in the rulemaking process. And that became my life's work over the last five years." Others reported similar transformations. Ruth, another cannabis business owner, told me, "The first time I went to any sort of political meeting, rally, anything, was around the cannabis business. . . . I wasn't politically active at all until this business. Now I'm part of every single advocacy group."

Many cannabis business owners feel that it is particularly important for them to get involved in cannabis activism, because they believe that the rules that are being put in place to regulate this industry are being written by people that have no real experience with cannabis. As a result, these rules often prove unworkable in practice. Ernest told me:

> These marketplaces are generally structured from a law, regulation, and policy perspective by people who don't know anything about cannabis, and who may have also previously been adamantly opposed to this substance. . . . It's a brand-new industry and there's going to have to be necessarily an evolution of the laws and rules at a pretty fast clip, but sometimes those changes don't really seem to make much sense, and certainly don't seem to really be aimed at helping the licensed operators themselves try to be more successful.

None of the cannabis business owners that I spoke with for this project had much of anything positive to say about the regulatory agencies overseeing cannabis in their state. This is not particularly surprising. We should expect some animosity between regulators, and the people working in the industry that they are regulating. But the relationship between cannabis business owners and their regulators seems especially caustic.

In Washington, for example, the Liquor and Cannabis Board (LCB) was given complete jurisdiction over the creation and enforcement of all regulatory rules governing cannabis. One activist complained that the LCB seemed less interested in creating a well-functioning industry and more interested in enforcement. She said, "They came out of the gate with an enforcement bent. Let's catch these people doing something wrong and stick it to them." This punitive stance alienated many cannabis business owners in the state. Jody spoke for many when she told me, "The liquor and cannabis board might actually be where government employees go to get tenure when they can't, like, stay in any other department. They are some of the worst human beings on the planet."

Instead of hiring regulators who have practical experience with cannabis, most states have followed Washington's lead and tasked bodies that were originally designed to regulate alcohol with overseeing this new industry. To be fair, this is what many cannabis activists themselves had been asking for during legalization campaigns. Oftentimes they did not even say the word "legalization," instead framing these laws as an attempt to "regulate cannabis like alcohol." But cannabis and alcohol are very different substances, with very different regulatory needs. For example, the hops and grains used in alcoholic beverages must be brewed or distilled before they become an intoxicating substance. This means that the agricultural side of the alcohol industry is generally treated as separate from the brewing, distillation, and distribution. This is not the case for the cannabis plant. As a result, many states that have legalized cannabis have treated the growing, processing, and sale of cannabis as part of the same industry. This can create technical problems for cannabis farmers. One cannabis farmer in Washington told me:

> It would have been nice if the initial legislation had required the [Washington State Department of Agriculture], folks who were familiar with agriculture . . . to play a more key role in regulating and supporting the industry. But the legislation didn't really involve the WSDA, it only involved the LCB. . . . There's no technical support available to the small farmers out here. I had a group of farmers in [one county] who were all having issues with cloning this

year. . . . The only place they can turn to is Google because they can't call up
. . . the Department of Ag to come and assist them.

The fact that the state created a regulatory agency without ensuring that it
had the technical expertise to assist the industry that it oversees suggests
that even lawmakers saw the LCB primarily as a punitive body.

Giving people from the cannabis community more oversight over the
cannabis industry is not just a practical matter, however. For many activists, it is also a moral one. Harriet told me:

> You've got to start listening to the people who kept cannabis alive all of these
> years through prohibition at risk to themselves, their families, their lives,
> their assets, their freedom. And now we're just allowing bureaucrats to make
> up the rules, to decide what adequate canopy is? To decide what adequate
> service is to patients? To decide the appropriate ratios of cannabinoids and
> which one is medical and which one is not? Are you kidding me? Logic has
> been largely absent in the cannabis wars.

The battle over cannabis regulation is about more than just how to create
the most efficient cannabis market possible. It is also about who gets to
be the primary beneficiary of cannabis legalization. Activists like Harriet
want to make sure that regulatory bodies enable those who fought the
hardest for cannabis reform, often at great personal risk, to benefit from
these laws.

Giving people from the cannabis community more influence over the
regulatory process could be a particularly effective way to advance goals
like racial equity. One way to make sure that the benefits of cannabis
legalization flow to people of color is to put people of color in charge of
designing these regulations. One activist told me:

> What we should do is go into each city and we should hire people of color
> . . . into our regulatory bodies. . . . We could give them a solid, world-class
> income, with health benefits. . . . If the drug war is about people of color espe-
> cially being targeted by enforcement, then giving people of color enforcement
> jobs is one way to kind of structurally reverse that. . . . [We] should really
> involve the communities that are affected. . . . Their voices have to be there.
> . . . What's the right thing to do? Let's ask the people who we're supposed to
> be trying to help.

In addition to helping build a more equitable cannabis industry, putting
more people of color in charge of regulation has economic benefits for

those individual regulators. Jody told me, "I keep telling the Black community, I'm like, 'You should go be enforcement. You should go regulate all the white people.' It's got a pension. It's not as sexy as owning a cannabis grow, but it's got a pension, it's got benefits, you've got tenure."

The Limits of Grassroots Organizing

Most of the small-business owners who got involved with cannabis reform after legalization had no prior history of political activism to draw from. Those who did have previous experience with activism were most familiar with the kind of grassroots volunteer organizing that had served the cannabis reform movement well during the fight over legalization. They leaned on that experience initially when trying to influence the regulatory rules governing legal cannabis markets. Catherine, for example, told me about her first attempt to alter zoning restrictions that were placed on cannabis farmers in Washington:

> The Washington State Association of Building Officials had put forth the proposal to classify marijuana cultivation as a moderate hazard factory industrial use. And what that would have done is triggered F-1 building code requirements for any building or structure where marijuana was grown. . . . You can't really make a greenhouse to F-1 code. . . . And so, it was leaning really away from rural farmers, away from small businesses and away from outdoor cultivators, toward an indoor warehouse model.

Catherine and her husband, who had planned to open a small outdoor cannabis farm in the state, viewed these new restrictions as an existential threat. They decided to fight back. She told me:

> My husband and I leaned on our community organizing skills and experience and we held two different meetings where we educated the impacted marijuana farmers in our county. We educated them on what the zoning ordinance said, how we could engage in the process, how to provide testimony, when the hearing was going to be, how to call your county commissioners, and what sort of things we should be saying to them. . . . We ended up getting them to pull that back. And I think we really surprised the Building Code Council with our response. I don't think they were used to having a full room at their hearings.

The fact that Catherine and the farmers that she mobilized won that particular battle shows that grassroots organizing can be quite powerful in a legislative or regulatory environment when used selectively.

But this grassroots approach has serious limitations. It is an exhausting and time intensive tactic. As such, it can be used effectively one or two times per legislative session at most, and only for really salient issues that clearly impact lots of people directly. Catherine told me:

> When it comes to grassroots organizing, especially during a legislative session, I can probably organize a couple hundred farmers to do something once during a legislative session. So I've got to be really mindful of what is that thing I'm going to target and rally the troops around because people don't have energy to be rallied. You can't rally the grassroots multiple times during a session, it's just not going to work. You can do it once.

Such an approach is unsuitable for smaller day-to-day changes. The problem for cannabis reform activists is that, once you get to the enforcement stage of legislative development, most changes are smaller, more incremental ones, unlikely to capture the enthusiasm of a broad array of volunteer activists.

Another problem is that many of these rule changes are done in private meetings that are not open to the public. This makes it hard for even the most engaged business owners to influence the regulatory rulemaking process. Ernest told me:

> The Liquor and Cannabis Board actually has a board of three board members who meet generally five times every two weeks. The thing about that is that only one of those meetings was being recorded and broadcast. . . . [So] there wasn't a lot of information getting out from the Washington State Liquor and Cannabis Board, even though we have really good sunshine laws here in Washington. . . . We recognized that getting that information out would be extremely helpful. . . . We've pursued trying to make that work . . . and doing consistent citizen engagement, citizen observation, of the governing processes for cannabis policymaking in this state.

This shadowy rulemaking process is extremely problematic for grassroots oriented activists because, they rely on public outrage to put political pressure on these officials. It is not a barrier for those organizations who seek to influence rulemaking through paid lobbyists, however. Instead of engaging in public pressure campaigns, these lobbyists use campaign contributions and leverage their existing relationships, to schedule one-on-one meetings with legislative officials, where they can wield their influence in private.

Even when grassroots advocacy groups win public concessions from legislative officials, they often find that those victories are diminished afterward by amendments that are crafted in private. Eric told me:

> [Businesses] had the funds to pay for [lobbyists]. A grassroots organization like mine who are just getting by on pure donations, we can't hire a lobbyist. We got to lobby for ourselves. . . . Only way you're going to get politicians to move is they have to fear that there's enough people to make a change. And we're bringing those numbers to them now. So, they listen for the most part, but then when they go behind their closed doors, it's politics as usual. . . . They smile in our face and they say, "we're partners," and "we love working with you guys," but . . . all the little sneaky deals that creep into a bill in that eleventh hour. That's why they're not trusted.

To overcome these barriers, cannabis reform activists must learn how to navigate the "unwritten rules" that govern the development of regulatory rulemaking. They often face a steep learning curve while doing so. Catherine, for example, complained that "nobody ever really pulled me aside and said, 'Hey [Catherine], you know how you're really supposed to do this? You're supposed to schedule a one-hour meeting with these people who are making these decisions. And then you're supposed to have these off-the-record conversations with them, and that's how you really influence change.'" Lobbyists and people who have a lot of experience working in a legislative environment, however, know these unwritten rules well. This puts activists with a grassroots organizing background at a distinct disadvantage. As a result, even highly motivated volunteer activists struggle to make headway once the debate over cannabis reform moves to the implementation stage.

The only way to counteract this lack of enthusiasm and expertise is to hire paid lobbyists. Terry, an activist in Michigan, told me, "the lesson here really is you got to pay people. I mean when volunteerism fails and there's still work left to be done, there has to be some form of financial compensation so that you can continue to advance your wishes and your goals. I think it's time to transition from an all volunteer army, so to speak, into a more paid, selected trade association type of a relationship." Indeed, there has been an uptick in the amount of paid lobbying power devoted to cannabis reform of late. Catherine herself has benefited from this transition. She told me:

> This last session I actually got to direct a lobbyist and so I got to see what a difference that makes. . . . In years past, I would read bills, and I would think of amendments that could be made to the bill that would improve it, and I would send a letter or an email to the bill's sponsor . . . and then kind of nothing would happen. And then this last session I had a lobbyist, and I'd look over the bill and I would say, "Okay, well, it needs to be changed here to be better for the farmers." And then that change would be made. But the lobbyist goes about it in a different way, he's there in Olympia and a lot of it's through having meetings and face-to-face conversations.

Lobbyists cost money, however, and smaller, more social justice–oriented business owners typically have a lot less to spend than large multistate corporate operators. This puts them at a huge disadvantage when it comes to fighting these regulatory battles.

Competing with Corporate Lobbying Power

Cannabis has quickly developed into a multibillion-dollar industry in the United States, with some analysts predicting that it could generate $35 billion in sales annually by 2025 (New Frontier Data 2020). The enormous profit potential of this new industry has attracted significant investment from the business sector. Large cannabis corporations like Curaleaf, Green Thumb Industries, Cresco Labs, and Trulieve have grown into large multistate-operators, worth billions of dollars. These companies have access to vast economic and legal resources, and they use this power to influence the regulatory rules that govern the cannabis industry.

In Washington, for example, much of the effort to shape the regulatory structure governing the cannabis industry has been led by the Washington Cannabusiness Association (WACA). WACA represents most of the big cannabis corporations in the state and was derisively referred to as "whacka" by many social justice–oriented activists. Jody told me, "[WACA] are all the big dogs, and they come to the government like they are lobbying for the cannabis community, but they're lobbying for themselves. And they don't care about their employees, and they are everything that's wrong with the industry. Everything." WACA speaks for only a small portion of the Washington cannabis industry, and its interests typically do not align with those of the smaller producers. But they have outsized influence over the regulatory process because, until very recently, they were the only organization that had the resources to pay lobbyists to influence the implementation process.

Many of the rule changes that WACA has pushed for run counter to the interests of smaller operators. For example, Washington is one of the only legal cannabis states that still has a robust residency requirement for cannabis business owners.[2] Residency requirements seek to protect local businesses by sheltering them from out-of-state competition. Most of the early cannabis legalization states included residency requirements as part of their legislation. But these restrictions have been fiercely opposed by corporate cannabis interests, because they make it difficult for large multistate operators to do business there. States like Oregon and Colorado have recently buckled to this pressure and repealed their residency requirements. Federal judges have struck them down as unconstitutional in other localities (Cioffi, Serratore, and Pinna 2021). This is alarming to many small-business owners in Washington, who view these restrictions as crucial to their survival. Ruth, told me:

> It's a scary thing to us that there's been serious talk about getting rid of residency requirements to allow out-of-state ownership to come into Washington. . . . If out-of-state ownership is allowed in this state, corporate influence is going to be a huge detriment to small businesses like ours. . . . They'll lobby to expand their license capacity, and it'll just squeeze out the mom and pops.

As Ruth points out, these rule changes bring financial benefits to large corporate operators who can then use this increased revenue to solidify their political power in the state. This makes it even harder to resist proposed rule changes in the future.

Ruth is right to worry. Similar things have happened in other legal cannabis states already. In California, for example, the state had initially imposed cultivation caps on cannabis growers. These caps were meant to limit the size of cannabis grow operations in order to give small growers a chance to compete equally with their larger, more well-resourced competitors. But these promised protections for small businesses quickly withered under the strain of corporate lobbying power. Henry recalled bitterly that:

> They promised us a one-acre cap. That meant that no cannabis cultivator could have a cannabis grow operation more than one acre. But big dispensaries such as Harborside . . . lobbied Sacramento and so the bureaucracy decided to lift the cap and so now there can be grows as big as you want them to be. We were promised a five-year moratorium on grows bigger than one acre and they reneged on that and so a lot of small cannabis providers are out of business.

In the absence of cultivation caps, small "craft growers" must grow premium products in order to have a chance at profitability. Large growers, on the other hand, can use economies of scale to drive down their price point, offering more affordable products to a wider market. This leaves small producers competing for a tiny segment of the cannabis industry, while the big producers enjoy the bulk of the profits (Allen 2022).

Trade organizations like WACA are not always able to successfully structure regulatory rules to their advantage, however. When these efforts fail, they typically switch tactics, pressuring legislative officials to treat large operators who have run afoul of existing regulations with more leniency. Ernest explains that many large operators in Washington faced mounting fees for regulatory infractions. Instead of paying those fees, however, they accused regulators of bias and successfully pushed for changes that could prevent them from being fined in the future:

> This last legislative session, there was actually a bill passed, SB-5318, which really was driven by that Washington Cannabusiness Association. It forced really a pretty substantial reorganization of the enforcement division at the Liquor and Cannabis Board upon the agency. One thing they focused on was what they called an inconsistency of enforcement, and inconsistent application of the rules. . . . [That] seems like it was driven in part by some of those large operators whose licenses had become at risk because of the accrual of violations over time.

Even in cases of clear rules violations, the mere threat of continual litigation can often pressure state actors, who do not have the resources to compete with these large corporate law firms indefinitely, to settle disputes over rules violations for far less than they are worth. Catherine explains:

> Washington has done a better job of preserving the market diversity than other states. But I think that they have pretty much met their limit as far as how much longer they can protect the small businesses, because it seems to me that the big guys have gotten so much money behind them now. And they

have their attorneys and they litigate, litigate, litigate and the state can only afford to litigate for so long. What I'm seeing now is they're settling these cases and it's more of a slap on the hand than anything else.

This arrangement effectively grants special treatment to large operators. Due to their size, legal resources, and lobbying power, these corporations are able to violate regulatory rules with relative impunity.

Smaller operators, who do not have the same resources, cannot do the same. This means that regulatory oversight hits them much harder than their larger competitors. Henry told me:

> We have equity applicants . . . who run retail cannabis businesses. They're expected to give up 10 percent of all their gross receipts to the city, which is choking them financially. They're dangling by a very slender thread. . . . It's been estimated by the California Growers Association that over half of the cannabis cultivators are now out of business because they are burned by the excessive regulations and fees and cannot afford to be in compliance. . . . So, cannabis regulations, in my humble opinion, are a mess in California. And they favor the big corporations.

This unequal enforcement process accelerates the consolidation of the cannabis industry, making it even more top-heavy than it was originally. As Henry points out, this dynamic is particularly problematic for people of color, who are almost always in the position of being smaller operators with limited resources. It is especially galling because these larger operators, who typically enjoy larger profits, have far more resources with which to pay for regulatory violations than their smaller competitors.

In addition to their monetary advantages, these companies are also able to draw on their experience navigating regulatory rules in other economic sectors and apply that to the cannabis industry. Large corporations typically have existing relationships with high-priced law firms who have considerable regulatory experience. These attorneys are able to comb through complex regulatory rules and find legal loopholes that can be exploited. For example, Washington still prohibits nonresidents from owning cannabis licenses. However, a recent amendment to that rule allows out-of-state ownership groups to finance cannabis corporations in Washington, so long as the actual named license holder is a local resident. This change has proven easy for multistate operators to exploit. Catherine told me:

> When they opened up financing for out of state . . . you could be a financier

in an unlimited number of businesses. And so, I think that's when we really started to see the big guys starting to control more licenses via financiers. So, what you'll see sometimes is . . . like big corporations out of Canada that are publicly traded on the stock exchange will come into Washington. And they may own the property and all of the assets of the business, but they aren't the licensee. . . . So, they were compliant, but definitely not within the intent of the law. They were figuring out a way to work in those gray areas of the law.

These large corporations are "repeat players," to borrow Mark Galanter's term (1974). This gives them a huge advantage over smaller companies who are typically "one shotters" with no previous regulatory experience to draw from. These repeat players are also able to endure short-term profit losses in order to win regulatory disputes that will benefit them in the long run. Smaller operators do not typically have the same luxury.

In an attempt to overcome these disadvantages, smaller producers in Washington banded together to form their own cannabis trade organization. The Cannabis Alliance is a collection of more than 300 mostly smaller operators in the state. They cannot match the resources of organizations like WACA, but their members are highly motivated, and they have been able to scrape together enough money to fund a lobbyist—most years anyway. Jody told me:

> The Cannabis Alliance, which is a grassroots movement [of small operators] that has been . . . just bootstrapping it since the beginning. . . . Our lobbyist has worked for free for the last year because we don't have any money, and he's like, "You guys are just so good. Everything about you is who I want to lobby for, but never get to." And we're like, "We will pay you; we just don't have it yet." There's a lot of goodness that can be had and a lot of hope in a world that doesn't have a lot of that right now.

The corporate domination of the cannabis industry has been a great disappointment for many activists. Despite their efforts to promote equity, it is likely that large corporations will be able to leverage their massive resources to their advantage. It is probably too late to prevent corporate domination of the cannabis industry. But efforts like those of the Cannabis Alliance are still important. They can help secure at least part of this industry for smaller operators. In this way, legal cannabis may develop similarly to the beer industry, where independently operated craft breweries made up a small, but significant, 13 percent of total market share in 2021 (Brewers Association 2021).

Making Meaning Out of Cannabis Activism

> [Activism] it's hard. You lose more than you win, it feels like. . . . [But] if I'm not going to do it, who is? You know? We've got to stick together with the people who have the same values and just keep fighting. Otherwise, if we don't, we're just giving up at that point, and then I really couldn't get up in the morning. You know what I'm saying?
> —Kimberly (cannabis activist)

In his 1971 book *Rules for Radicals*, esteemed community organizer Saul Alinsky reflects on a lifetime spent engaging in social movement activism. Speaking to a new generation of aspiring young activists he describes their task thusly, "If we think of the struggle as a climb up a mountain, then we must visualize a mountain with no top. We see a top, but when we finally reach it, the overcast rises and we find ourselves merely on a bluff. . . . And so it goes on, interminably" (21). Many activists will find the interminable nature of their task exhausting, even demoralizing, at least at times. Cannabis activists could be forgiven for feeling a little like the mythical Sisyphus at the moment, rolling a boulder up a hill, only to watch it roll back down shortly afterward. In the face of such challenges, many have become disenchanted.

Alinsky, however, views this metaphor as hopeful. He says, "Unlike the chore of the mythic Sisyphus . . . we are always going further upward. . . . At times we do fall back and become discouraged, but it is not that we are making no progress. . . . The pursuit of happiness is never-ending; happiness lies in the pursuit" (1971, 22). Of course, as a man who dedicated his life to activism, it behooved Alinsky to maintain such a positive outlook. Helping members make meaning out of their activism is central to the project of any good community organizer. Few people are willing to risk legal consequences, loss of employment, physical harm, or even just waste their leisure time working on behalf of a movement that they believe to be unimportant or doomed to fail.

Leadership plays a central role in helping to set the tone and boost morale in times of struggle. Eric told me, "I have to stay optimistic for my members, because every day I come in there and it's doom and gloom and stuff like that, then that's what they're going to feel. So, we got to uplift . . . fight for the things that is right. And at the end of the day, even if we don't win, we know we did the right thing. And that's what we're doing." Maintaining a positive attitude during times of struggle is no small task. Activism is a grind, and the reality is that sometimes movement leaders do not feel particularly motivated or hopeful. In times like these, activists must find a way to take satisfaction from fighting hard for a righteous cause, even if they ultimately do not accomplish all of their goals.

Adopting such a perspective is easier if activists have a selective memory, savoring the wins while quickly forgetting the losses. Michael, a longtime drug reform activist, epitomized this mentality. When asked to reflect on his career as an activist, he told me, "What I'm doing is important work. I don't hit a home run every day. Hell, I don't hit a single every day. I strike out most days. My batting average as a baseball player would be like you wouldn't pay me 10 cents, but overall, I've swung that bat 1,001 times and I've gotten a few hits and it's making a difference in people's lives, so there you go." But a lifetime of struggle takes its toll, even on the most resilient of activists. Michael also told me, "I'm sixty-eight years old. I'm down to about thirty hours a week. I just don't have the psychic power. . . . It takes a lot of mental energy to go into the swamp every day and fight the dragons and the alligators, and now it just drains me, so I can only handle about two days, sometimes three days a week. That's it."

Mustering the psychic power to handle the inevitable defeats may be easier for younger activists, especially if they are able to put their actions into a larger context. Nathan, a youth activist, told me:

> We always understand that we are playing against a tough field right now. . . . [But] we know that the tide of history is on our side. At this point, we know that it's not a question of if, but when, and we're just trying to make that when as soon as possible. . . . We understand that sometimes we're not going to win, but just knowing that we might have lost this battle, but we're not going to lose the war, that keeps us reassured that we can just keep going.

Nathan's vision of himself as playing a small part in a larger fight for cannabis reform insulates him from disappointment. Neither Nathan nor

Michael sees themselves as messianic figures who must lead their people to the promised land. Instead, they are playing a small part in a larger drama. This highlights the multigenerational nature of the cannabis reform project. Younger activists like Nathan, who may have more enthusiasm and energy, will need to pick up the baton from more seasoned activists like Michael, who grow understandably tired after decades of struggle.

As with any movement, people join the fight for cannabis reform because they believe in the righteousness of this cause. But people typically stay with movements long-term for more practical reasons. Many simply get a lot of personal enjoyment out of their work. Michael, who rose to a prominent position with a major national drug reform organization, continued doing activism in part because he found his work exhilarating. He told me, "When I got [to DC] in '06, I'm in Congress four or five days a week. I'm up at sixty, seventy hours a week because, one, I love it, and two, I'm working in the United States Congress! . . . You're in the big show, and it's a pretty cool feeling." Beulah told me something similar, "Being involved in policy reform has changed my life because of the opportunities that it's given me, and the direction that it's brought to me in my life. I've gotten to do amazing things like speak at the White House, big conventions, and change people's lives, and see amazing things."

Others gravitated toward activism because it gave their life a sense of purpose and meaning that they did not have otherwise. Byron is a young activist who was drawn to the cause of drug reform by his personal experience growing up in a family that was touched powerfully by the War on Drugs. He told me, "My father got arrested [on drug charges] back in the '80s. . . . They sentenced him to fifteen years and then he got kicked out of the country. This was when I was a young baby, so I barely remember him. . . . So, my personal reason [for activism] is this war on drugs." Byron faced a lot of hardships growing up without a father. As a young man he was a little lost and found himself on the wrong side of the law at times. He credits his activism with giving him a sense of purpose in life. He told me:

> I'm trying to . . . influence a young [Byron], that you can make a change. Do not dull the pain with drugs. Do not try to hide away from the facts of wherever you come from. If you feel something is off, if you feel like something's not right, be vocal, have a voice, a structured voice, because you could be the

catalyst to major changes. I feel like that's what [my activism] has allowed me to do. It has allowed me to find my voice and see what I'm fighting for. When I wake up in the morning and I don't want to do anything, I just think of that and hopefully when I'm older, some kid tells me, "hey I saw you one time and you know, you changed my life and thank you so much." That's giving me goosebumps saying that. That's what keeps on pushing me.

The intrinsic value of activism is something that has long been noted by community organizers. Alinsky himself remarked that even when a campaign achieves none of its policy goals, if it gives the people who engaged in that campaign a sense of purpose, then those efforts were not in vain. As he puts it, "Through the organization and its power he will get his birth certificate for life, that he will become known, that things will change from the drabness of a life where all that changes is the calendar. . . . Suddenly he's alive! This is part of the adventure, part of what is so important to people in getting involved in organizational activities" (1971, 121).

CONCLUSION

Cannabis and the American Racial Imagination

The original cannabis community, are really amazing people, right? They believe in love, they believe in equality, they believe in a little bit of rebellion. They're pretty funky. . . . We could [change] the way capitalism is done in America where we could show instead of just caring about bottom-line profits, you could care about the environment and your community and your employees. . . . However, now being in the legal industry . . . we're competing with millionaires . . . all they want is money, money, money. And that is pushing back on really the soul of the plant and where we all come from and what it could do.
—Jody (cannabis business owner and activist)

We've been screwed by the wealthy, corporate interests who have no interest in medical cannabis. . . . All it's about is how much fucking money they can make. Excuse my language. But that's all they fucking care about, is how much money they can make.
—Henry (cannabis activist)

The times they are a-changing. Now that we have legalization, people are willing to admit that they're consumers . . . It's gone from tie-dye to suit and tie.
—Cecil (cannabis activist)

This book tells how cannabis went from being a strictly prohibited and heavily stigmatized substance to a commercial commodity that can be purchased legally in many US states. These findings suggest a number of potential avenues for future scholarly inquiry, and also offer lessons for those activists, public officials, and regular citizens, who seek to shape the future of cannabis reform. This concluding chapter provides an overview of the central insights of this research and then turns to some lingering questions raised by this inquiry.

Cannabis has been legalized in many US states, but it remains difficult for people who had been working in the illicit or medical cannabis marketplace to transition to the legal cannabis industry, foreclosing opportunities to use cannabis reform for progressive social change. As the epigraphs at the beginning of this chapter demonstrate, many longtime cannabis activists experienced these events as akin to a "hostile takeover" of the cannabis community by the corporate sector. There are indeed good reasons to be concerned about the outsized influence that corporations have had on the development of legal cannabis. Many activists struggled for years to influence cannabis reform in their state, only to be pushed aside during cannabis legalization campaigns in favor of more "professional" operatives, usually at the behest of corporate sponsors. Many states adopted business friendly cannabis laws, which did very little to address issues of racial equity or social justice, as a result.

But a focus on the influence of corporate interests only tells part of the story. In the second half of this conclusion, I complicate this narrative somewhat by taking a deeper look at the values of the "original" cannabis community that many feel is being replaced. Cannabis first came into the American popular consciousness during the Jazz Age. It became a part of mainstream youth culture during the 1960s and 1970s, thanks in large part to its association with the American counterculture, and its greatest cultural contribution—rock music. It was the counterculture that helped nurture the idea of cannabis as a symbol of rebellion, and it was members of the counterculture who formed the first cannabis activist organizations in the 1970s, sparking the modern cannabis reform movement. As such, I use 1960s counterculture as a stand in for the original cannabis community. I argue that a least part of the reason that corporate cannabis has been so successful, is that this community has never really been as progressive, or as hostile to corporate America as the stereotypical "hippie" image might lead us to believe. This is particularly true for race. Cannabis has always been framed in racially problematic ways, not just by the forces of prohibition, but also by the cannabis community itself.

Perhaps no one better demonstrated the difficulties of navigating race, capitalism, and cannabis in modern America than Robert Nesta Marley. "Bob" Marley and the Wailers first broke through in the United States with the album *Burnin'* in 1973. Initially, the American media portrayed Marley in explicitly racist terms, often depicting him as an ignorant rustic, a stoned-out street tough, a sex-crazed maniac, or a militant revolutionary. This highly racialized image helped endear Marley to the American counterculture, I argue, precisely because it allowed them to act out long standing racial fantasies. As a result, Marley developed a dedicated following with the primarily white rock music audience in the United States, but he never really broke through with African American listeners. Following his death from cancer in 1981, a concerted effort was made to revitalize Marley's public image and broaden his appeal to a more mainstream audience. Beginning with the issuing of *Legend* in 1984, Marley was increasingly portrayed as a unifying figure of peace and racial harmony. This resulted in an extremely lucrative period of his career, with album sales far in excess of anything Marley was able to achieve while alive. But this sanitized portrayal was once again more concerned with servicing the evolving post-racial fantasies of Marley's still primarily white American fan base, than authentically representing the anticolonial project of Black liberation that was so central to his music.

I offer Marley as a cautionary tale for those who seek to use cannabis to pursue progressive social change in the United States. Artists like Marley show the limits of working to advance political causes within the corporate space, particularly when those causes put you at odds with the economic interests of wealthy white people. Marley's experience suggests that Black people can succeed in this environment, but only by rendering their Blackness less visible, and only if they are willing to abandon the mission of racial egalitarianism for platitudes about diversity and racial harmony. This virtually guarantees that our efforts to improve racial equity in cannabis will never advance beyond the elevation of a few token representatives of the Black community, so long as it remains entrenched in the American capitalist system. In light of this history, the racially exploitative manner in which cannabis legalization has played out in the United States should not be viewed as aberrational. Instead, it should be seen as a continuation of the complicated racial dynamics that have always been central to the American counterculture, and the mostly white New Left activists who identified with it.

If we want to help move cannabis policy in a more progressive direction, then we need to be honest about the ways in which racism is baked into our capitalist economic system, and we need to make sure that our laws governing cannabis accurately reflect the diverse needs of the entire cannabis community. If we want our cannabis laws, and, I might argue, our larger efforts at racial justice, to be truly equitable, then we must do as so many earlier advocates of racial justice, including Marley himself, have suggested, and fuse our efforts for racial equity with the cause of economic justice (Du Bois 1935; King 1968). This means an increased willingness to look beyond the capitalist marketplace for solutions to seemingly intractable problems like racial and economic inequality.

Pot for Profit

> If the words "life, liberty and the pursuit of happiness" don't include the right to experiment with your own consciousness, then the Declaration of Independence isn't worth the hemp it was written on.
> —Terence McKenna

> Of course I know how to roll a joint.
> —Martha Stewart

Cannabis has received an uptick in scholarly attention of late, with hundreds of interdisciplinary "cannabis studies" programs forming at colleges and universities across the United States (Avetisian and Stone 2022). This influx of research suggests that cannabis studies is an emerging field of academic research centering on the cannabis plant, the people who care about it, and the intellectual, social, and cultural contexts that give meanings to it (see, for example, Corva and Meisel 2022). Yet sociolegal scholars have, until this point, largely ignored cannabis (but see: Aviram 2015, 78–97; Garriott 2020). This is perplexing because, as this book has demonstrated, law is central to the project of cannabis reform. In this section of the conclusion, I provide an overview of the scholarly contributions of this book, with an emphasis on drawing fruitful connections between cannabis and sociolegal studies.

Cannabis, Law, and Social Change

One of the foundational questions of sociolegal scholarship is, can law be an effective mechanism for bringing about social change? The scholarly literature on law and social change developed in the aftermath of the "Rights Revolution," and was primarily focused on understanding the long-term impact of progressive court decisions like *Brown v. Board of Education* (1954) (see, for example, Scheingold 1974; Rosenberg 1991; McCann 1994). Cannabis reform, on the other hand, emerged as a political issue during a time in which the American judiciary has become increasingly overtaken by the conservative legal movement. As such, cannabis reform activists have tended to bypass courts, in favor of more promising avenues of change. Indeed, *Gonzales v. Raich* (2005), the most high-profile cannabis case to ever come before the US Supreme Court, offered a powerful rebuke to the medical cannabis movement. In a 6–3 decision, the court invalidated California's medical cannabis law, declaring that the ultimate power to regulate cannabis rests with the federal government, not the states.

As far as the US Supreme Court is concerned, everyone who is currently participating in the legal cannabis industry is operating in brazen defiance of federal law. Yet *Raich,* which has never been overturned, has done nothing to stop the cannabis reform movement. If anything cases like *Raich* were only used by cannabis activists to illustrate the dangers of prohibition and emphasize the need for more substantive reforms (Hecht 2014, 106–37). As support for cannabis continued to rise among the American public, government officials were forced to choose between obeying *Raich*, or obeying the will of their voters. Many states chose to legalize cannabis, rendering *Raich* irrelevant without even bothering to overturn the precedent. This suggests that legal change comes not from the top down, but from the bottom up, a concept that some scholars have termed "popular constitutionalism" (Schmidt 2018).

This increased popular support for cannabis did not happen by accident. In chapter 2, I showed how cannabis became more socially acceptable as it became associated with elements of American society that enjoy more cultural sway, particularly upper- and middle-class white people in the business community. This was often done quite explicitly by members of the cannabis reform movement, who elevated the visibility of the more "respectable" elements of the cannabis community, while working to limit the visibility of others. These "neoliberal respectability politics" may very well have aided the cannabis reform movement's efforts to build support for legalization. It also ensured that legalizationplayed out in ways that primarily benefited these "responsible" members of the cannabis community, often to the detriment of others.

This analysis demonstrates the value of disentangling the scholarly concepts of "frame" and "culture," two ideas that are frequently conflated by social scientists (Oliver and Johnston 2000). In this book, I have shown how a movement goes about constructing *frames* of communication within the context of a dominant political *culture* of neoliberalism. Every movement that has emerged in the United States since at least the 1980s has had to navigate this terrain. The ones that have been most successful at shifting public opinion in their favor have largely done so by espousing neoliberal principles. The Gay Rights Movement, for example, often presented gay people as white, upper-middle-class professionals, seeking to form traditional nuclear family arrangements that conform to heteronormative ideals (Murray 2012; Franke, 2015; Mello 2016a, 136–46). Similarly, cannabis reform activists have sought to present cannabis users as responsible individuals who are deserving of rights, by framing them as diligent parents, responsible consumers, or savvy business professionals (Schlussel 2017; Kaufman 2022).

In this way, widespread cultural assumptions, such as the unquestioned wisdom of neoliberal economic principles, powerfully shape the trajectory of efforts to bring about social change. At times these cultural beliefs operate as an accelerant, providing "windows of opportunity" that allow savvy social movement organizers to push for social changes that improve the lives of at least some members of these communities. But the scope of change that is possible is also tightly constrained by the cultural norms of a given society (Mello 2016b). As a result, more radical social justice–oriented activists are often forced to choose between staying true to their values and achieving no change at all, or compromising some of their principles in order to implement more modest reforms.

Indeed, many of the activists that I interviewed for this study complained about being asked to support cannabis legislation that they believed to be deeply flawed. These concerns are particularly resonant for people of color, who have a long history of being told to swallow flawed legislation and "fix it later." Pragmatic activists often plead with others, "don't let the perfect be the enemy of the good." They argue that enacting a flawed bill is better than no bill at all, because it can always be reformed later. But as we saw in chapter 4, cannabis legalization creates powerful new stakeholders who have a strong interest in preserving the status quo, limiting the prospects for change. This suggests that activists looking to use cannabis reform to generate social change should push aggressively for legalization bills that put progressive values at the forefront, rather than accepting flawed cannabis legislation, in the hopes of reforming it later.

Legal Cannabis on the Books versus the Law in Action

Concerns about the unintended consequences of flawed cannabis legislation proved to be well founded. As we saw in chapter 3, the benefits of legalization have not been felt by all members of the cannabis community equally. Steep barriers to entry make it difficult for those without legitimate business experience and access to capital to have success in the legal cannabis industry. These new regulations are justified by the logic of the market, which makes them seem like race neutral, merit-based restrictions, but they replicate the same patterns of privilege that are seen in other segments of the US economy. Those who are unable to enter the legal cannabis space are forced to either leave the cannabis trade entirely, or continue operating in the illicit marketplace after legalization, even though doing so risks arrest. This demonstrates a common concern of sociolegal scholarship—that there is a persistent gap between the law as it appears on the books and the law as it behaves in action (Calavita 2016, 109–34).

Even in states where cannabis is supposedly "legal," there are still a myriad of laws dictating how the drug must be purchased, transported, and consumed. These laws are often used by police officers as a pretext for stopping, interrogating, and even arresting people, particularly people of color (Garriot 2020; Polson 2022). Though arrests for cannabis offenses have dropped considerably in states where cannabis has been legalized, they have not gone away. Indeed, in many states the gap between the cannabis arrest rate for Black and white people has actually grown since legalization (ACLU 2020, 36). Nonstate actors like landlords, employers, and neighborhood associations also have the power to restrict cannabis use, even when it has been legalized in their state. These restrictions disproportionately impact poor people and people of color, who are less likely to be viewed as responsible cannabis users, more likely to work in fields that are subjected to workplace drug testing, and have lower rates of homeownership (Bender 2016, 700–704).

The impact of being denied access to legal cannabis is more significant than many realize. Illicit cannabis was a lifeline for many people who, for one reason or another, found themselves on the outside of the capitalist economic system. As the legal industry grows, and illicit cannabis becomes more untenable, entire communities are likely to lose their livelihoods. The growth of the corporate cannabis industry comes at the expense of illicit operators like Todd and communities like Guy's, who depend on illicit cannabis for support. Many of these people have no other legitimate means of making money available to them. Without cannabis dollars, life in these communities is likely to get more desperate.

The Evolving Legal Consciousness of Cannabis

How do average citizens navigate this gap between the promise of cannabis law and the reality of it? These types of questions have long motivated sociolegal scholars interested in understanding the "legal consciousness" of average citizens (Silbey 2005). For some, cannabis legalization has been a positive experience. As we saw in chapter 2, legalizing cannabis has reduced the stigma associated with the drug, allowing many longstanding members of the cannabis community to feel comfortable stepping out of the "cannabis closet." Law conveys powerful moral legitimacy in the modern United States (Tyler 1990; Glendon 1993). As such, legalizing cannabis allows at least some members of the cannabis community to be recognized as responsible citizens who are deserving of rights, granting them immense relief.

Of course, not everyone has had the same overwhelmingly positive experience with cannabis legalization. People like Todd or Harriet who find themselves excluded from the legal cannabis industry, tend to have a much more confrontational view of cannabis law. Some embraced their outlaw status, gaining a sense of legitimacy, not from the law, but from the righteousness of their struggle against it. This gave them the motivation to continue fighting in the face of resistance. Even activists who reported feeling frustrated with the slow pace of change, still gained enormous symbolic benefits from participating in a cause that felt so meaningful to them.

Cannabis, Race, and the American Counterculture

> I walked with every muscle aching among the lights of 27th and Welton in the Denver colored section, wishing I were a Negro, feeling that the best the white world had offered was not enough ecstasy for me. . . . I wished I were a Denver Mexican, or even a poor overworked Jap, anything but what I was so drearily, a "white man" disillusioned.
> —Jack Kerouac, *On the Road* (1957, 179)

How did we get to this point with cannabis legalization? For many of the longtime cannabis activists that I interviewed for this project, the blame lies primarily with the outsized influence of corporate cannabis. As I have demonstrated, there are indeed good reasons to be concerned about the way that corporations have shaped the development of legal cannabis. But a focus on the influence of corporate interests only tells part of the story. In this section of this conclusion, I complicate this narrative somewhat by taking a deeper look at the values of the "original" cannabis community that many feel is being replaced—the American counterculture.

Perhaps no movement cast a longer shadow over modern American life than 1960s counterculture. During this period "hippies" flocked to urban enclaves like San Francisco, forming communities that shunned the trappings of middle-class life, in pursuit of a more "authentic" and morally pure existence (Rossinow 1998). What exactly it meant to live authentically was never well articulated, but counterculture author, and occasional cannabis activist Hunter S. Thompson got close to capturing the spirit of the era when he wrote, "San Francisco in the middle sixties was a very special time and place to be a part of. Maybe it *meant something*. Maybe not, in the long run . . . but no explanation, no mix of words or music or memories can touch that sense of knowing that you were there and alive in that corner of time and the world. Whatever it meant" (1971, 66–67).

Whatever it meant to be a part of the counterculture at that time, one thing is clear—cannabis was a big part of it. As Thompson's quote suggests, the hippies and their predecessors the beatniks were less interested in accomplishing political goals, and more intoxicated with what historian Grace Hale calls the "romance of the outsider" (Hale 2011). Yet, these overwhelmingly white, relatively affluent, typically college-educated, young people had little occasion to experience being an outsider in their everyday lives. As we saw in chapter 1, smoking cannabis, which was both illegal and highly stigmatized at the time, allowed them to experience the titillation of violating not only the law, but also the established cultural norms of the day. As Yippie activist Jerry Rubin once proudly declared, "smoking pot makes you a criminal and a revolutionary" (as quoted in Booth 2003). For the young people who identified with the counterculture during this era, that was precisely the point of smoking it!

White Negros

For young white Americans growing up during the 1950s and 1960s, no one embodied the romance of being an outsider more than people of color, especially Black people. During this time, white teens began embracing "Black" fashion, slang, habits, and of course Black music—especially jazz, blues, and later, rock and roll (Hale 2011, 49–131). Since cannabis was first introduced to the American public by Mexican laborers and Black jazz musicians (see chapter 1), many saw their decision to smoke it in explicitly racial terms as well. Milton "Mezz" Mezzrow, for example, would use his close friendship with Louis Armstrong to become one of the most prominent cannabis dealers of the Jazz Age. Mezz, a white man of Jewish ancestry, described his decision to embrace this "outlaw" lifestyle in explicitly racial terms, remarking that he had "rejected white society and vowed to become a Negro" (as quoted in Lee 2012, 44). In this way, smoking cannabis allowed young white Americans to engage in a kind of racial cosplay. As historian Doug Rossinow writes, "African American culture was a repository of authenticity, which spiritually desiccated whites might tap through a kind of racial 'crossover'" (1998, 15).

For a time, this cultural affinity bred a type of political affinity as well, with many young northern whites gravitating toward the cause of racial justice. As the most culturally significant social movement of its day (perhaps ever) the civil rights movement was highly romanticized by many white activists. Tom Hayden, president of Students for a Democratic Society (SDS), one of the most prominent New Left activist organizations of this time, said that Black activists engaging in the civil rights movement, "lived a fuller level of feeling than any people I'd ever seen. . . . I wanted to live like them" (as quoted in Hale 2011, 2). Hayden and many of his compatriots did live like them, at least for a while. He helped to build fruitful connections between the overwhelmingly white SDS, which had emerged on college campuses in the north, and the Student Nonviolent Coordinating Committee (SNCC), which originated in Southern HBCUs, and was primarily composed of Black activists (Schmidt 2018). He was arrested for marching with the Freedom Riders in 1961, spending his birthday in jail (Rossinow 1998, 165). He later helped found the Mississippi Summer Project, better known as "Freedom Summer," in which white college students from the North came to Mississippi, working closely with organizations like SNCC to register Black voters and advocate for racial equality (Hale 2011, 189–203).

But these political alliances were always tenuous. Many of the white people who joined these movements were more interested in having a good time than actually advancing the cause of racial justice. This led some to question the sincerity of white activists, who spoke the language of racial equity, but seemed unwilling to make the sacrifices that were required to achieve these goals (King 1963). At the same time, a new generation of Black activists was coming of age, many of whom had been influenced by the Black Power movement. In his widely read 1966 essay in the *New York Review of Books,* Stokley Carmichael, who had just taken over leadership of SNCC from John Lewis, offered pointed criticisms of white "allies." He writes, "These are people supposedly concerned about Black Americans, but today they think first of themselves. . . . Too many young middle-class Americans . . . have wanted to come alive through the Black community.

They've wanted to be where the action is—and the action has been in the Black community" (Carmichael 1966).

This led to a splintering of progressive activists along racial lines. White activists agreed to step down from the SNCC, which had an integrated staff at the time, in December of 1966. The SDS moved away from the cause of racial equity, becoming increasingly focused on opposition to the Vietnam War. Many in the counterculture, which had always been over-whelmingly white, began engaging in what some have termed "cultural activism" (Rossinow 1998, 247). Groups like the "Diggers," the "Yippies," and the "Merry Pranksters" sought change, not through the political pro-cess, but through unconventional means such as establishing communes, using psychedelic drugs to promote "consciousness expansion," or engag-ing in performance art. Some of these cultural activists began organizing for cannabis reform, creating the first formal cannabis activist organiza-tions (see chapter 1). These activists were all white, and nearly all male, a legacy that continues to impact cannabis reform efforts today.

Cultural spaces were becoming more segregated at this time as well. Rock music was originally created by Black artists like Chuck Berry and Bo Diddley, who were themselves drawing on a larger tradition of Black blues musicians. But it came to be seen by the American public as a "white" genre during this period. This was thanks in part to the influence of British bands like the Beatles, and especially the Rolling Stones. These bands honed their sound by listening to African American blues and rock artists, before traveling across the pond to play for massive audiences of enraptured white American teenagers. The American media dubbed this the "British Invasion," helping to reimagine rock music as a primarily white genre. Rock critics and record companies nurtured this racial segre-gation, ghettoizing Black artists in far less lucrative subgenres like "soul" or "gospel," while simultaneously categorizing nearly all white artists of the era as "rock" (Hamilton 2016). By the time Jimi Hendrix burst onto the scene with his legendary performance at the Monterey Pop Festival in 1967, rock had become so entrenched as a "white" genre in the American consciousness that some critics dismissed him as an "Uncle Tom." They could not understand why a Black man was playing "white" music for a predominately white audience (Murray 1989, 78–105; Hamilton 2016, 213–45).

Tuff Gong

The fraught racial legacy of the American counterculture poses continued challenges for those who seek to navigate the cannabis space today. Perhaps no one better demonstrates these difficulties than Bob Marley. Marley was born in Nine Miles Jamaica in 1945. He was named after his father, a white man whom he met only a handful of times as a youth. At the age of twelve he moved with his mother to the Kingston slums of Trenchtown. They lived in abject poverty, sharing a tiny shack with no electricity or running water, and often going hungry. It was during this period that Marley first fell in love with the streets. To his mother's horror, he began dressing, talking, and acting like the "rude boys" (street toughs) she saw on the corners. His prowess as a street fighter earned him the nickname "Tuff Gong," and he was reputed to be quick with a switchblade (White 2006, 118–43).

Marely became enthralled with Kingston's vibrant music scene beginning with ska, then rocksteady, and eventually reggae. The slower tempo and syncopated beats that are characteristic of reggae give the music a relaxed, pacific vibe to many listeners today, but the violence is barely contained below the surface. Indeed, it often was not contained at all. Fights between rude boys and police were common at Wailers shows, leading many of the city's dance Halls to consider banning them due to the "criminal element" that they attracted (White 2006, 198). It was not just the fans who were violent, the Wailers were not afraid to deploy violence themselves when necessary. Marley's tour manager Allan Cole recalled, "For us to get airplay, we had to put a lot of strength, what you call muscle, to get played from the various disc jockeys, and things like that. So it was my duty to see that these things happened. . . . Occasionally we had to beat—we had to beat disc jockeys. We had to send guys to—smash their cars or things like that. Threaten them" (as quoted in White 2006, 373).

In 1968 Marley converted to Rastafarianism, a Jamaican folk religion that blends the Pan-African political beliefs of Jamaican activist Marcus Garvey, and the teachings of the "Holy Piby" or "Black man's Bible." Rastafarianism preaches a doctrine of political engagement and Black liberation. It resonated most strongly with the lower classes and was especially popular in the ghettos of Kingston. Most upper- and middle-class Jamaicans, on the other hand, despised this strange cult. They were appalled by the ragged appearance of the Rasta's dreadlocks, their subversive political views, and especially their near-constant use of "ganja" (cannabis), which was illegal in Jamaica at the time (White 2006, 13–16). Marley's embrace of Rastafarianism sent a strong message to everyone in Jamaica that he was on the side of the "sufferahs."

The Wailers were a hit in Jamaica beginning in the mid-1960s, but they did not break out in the United States until after signing with Island Records in 1972. They quickly released two albums *To Catch a Fire* (1973) and *Burnin'* (1973). *Burnin'* ended up being their breakthrough album. It was the last album that Marley made with the original Wailers lineup of Peter Tosh and Bunny Wailer. It was also one of the last true reggae albums that the band produced, as Marley would turn more toward pop music in his later years. The album is one of the most political that the band ever recorded. "Get Up Stand Up" often appears on lists of the greatest protest songs of all time, calling on listeners to take responsibility for their own lives and seek to better themselves, while also taking a few shots at organized religion. "Small Axe" is another great, multilayered protest song, with the axe working as a partial metaphor for Marley's own guitar, a suggestion that the Wailers' music itself could be a tool for liberation.

There are strong undertones of violence throughout this album. "I Shot the Sheriff," which Marley later revealed had originally been titled "I Shot the Police," but was changed to appease record producers (Uitti 2022), is an obvious example.[2] But the most explosive song on the album is undoubtedly "Burnin' and Lootin'." It opens with a chilling scene of authoritarian terror:

> This morning I woke up in a curfew
> Oh, God, I was a prisoner too, yeah!
> Could not recognize the faces standing over me
> They were all dressed in uniforms of brutality, Ay!

Before culminating with a call to resist violently:

> (That's why we gonna be)
> Burnin' and a-lootin' tonight
> (I Say we gon' to burn and loot)

Burnin' and a-lootin' tonight
(One more thing)
Burnin' all pollution tonight
(Oh, yeah, yeah)
Burnin' all illusion tonight

The album art was just as controversial as the music itself. The back of the album featured an artistic rendering of a dreadlocked Marley smoking a massive conical "joint" of cannabis, and the album included many full color photos of Black men in Kingston sporting dreadlocks and smoking large amounts of cannabis. Marley's embrace of cannabis was authentic, Rastafarians consider the plant sacred, and smoke it daily for spiritual enlightenment. Broadcasting his cannabis use so brazenly was also strategic, helping to cement him as a militant revolutionary, and build an audience with the white rock music fans in the counterculture. Cannabis was a big part of the rock scene, due to its status as a symbol of youth rebellion (Lee 2012, 103). Indeed, another Black musician, Jimi Hendrix, helped endear himself to the white counterculture with hits like "Purple Haze" and "The Wind Cries Mary," to name a few.

This message was received, *Burnin'* caused a furor. Marley biographer Timothy White explains how the American press initially reacted to the album:

> A lot of people believed that a Mau Mau-inspired cult of demonic antiwhite murderers had been uncovered in the Caribbean. The music conjured up images of white tourists being hacked to death on the fringes of tropical golf courses. . . . The American press . . . began running long, detailed pieces on this Jamaican cult that . . . smoked more pot than the populations of Haight-Asbury and Greenwich Village combined. It was a good story . . . falling right in line with the rest of the cult stories they'd been uncovering: the Mason family, the Lyman family, the Children of God, the acid churches, the suburban witch covens. (White 2006, 261)

This image of Marley repeats many of the same troupes of Black people as primitive savages that people like Norman Mailer were espousing in the 1950s. As Charles Shaar Murray has observed, Black artist hold the "accumulated weight of the fantasies and mythologies constructed around Black music and Black people by whites, hipsters and reactionaries alike . . . Black people represent the personification of the untrammeled id—intrinsically wild, sensual, dangerous, 'untamed'" (Murray 1989, 78). These images of Marley remained pretty much unchanged until after his death. Toward the end of his life Marley complained to his biographer that most reporters still treated him as "a novelty figure or a noble savage, surprised he could read, write or express himself beyond expounding on biblical tracts" (White 2006, 447).

As Marley's star grew brighter, he began getting pulled into the tumultuous Jamaican political scene, resulting in an assassination attempt in 1976. The exact details of the plot to kill Marley are still unknown, but the consensus seems to be that it was indeed politically motivated, most likely orchestrated by members of the Jamaica Labour Party (JLP). Marley was lucky to have survived the assault; a bullet entered his chest just below his heart and lodged itself in his arm. Two days later a wounded but defiant Marley performed a free "Smile Jamaica" concert as scheduled, with one arm in a sling, and Jamaican president Michael Manley, leader of the People's National Party (PNP), watching from the sidelines.

Following the show, a clearly shaken Marley went into self-imposed exile for the next two years. He traveled first to Nassau, where a "freaked" airport policemen asked if he was seeking "political asylum?" before being reassured that Marley was just there as "a tourist" (White 2006, 337). He later decamped to London, where he recorded two albums that would have outsized influence on his posthumous portrayals—*Exodus* (1977) and *Kaya* (1978). In the pantheon of Marley albums, *Kaya* and *Exodus* stand out as aberrational for their soft tone, emphasis on love songs, and near total lack of political engagement. In songs like "Satisfy My Soul" Marley seem to go out of his way to avoid engaging in politics, singing, "Oh, please don't you rock my boat/ (Don't rock my boat)/ 'Cause I don't want my boat to be rocking/ (Don't rock my boat)."

If anyone thought that Marley had lost his taste for political revolution though, *Survival* (1979) put those fears to rest. The album presents Marley as a mature revolutionary. Unlike the unfocused, chaotic violence of *Burnin'*, here violence is mustered purposefully, as a tool for third world liberation. The apotheosis of this is "Zimbabwe," a song Marley wrote in support of the Zimbabwe Independence Movement, a decades-long struggle to free the nation from colonial rule, which culminated in the election of Robert Mugabe in 1980. Songs like "So Much Trouble in this World," where Marley warns "what goes around comes around," tell a story of colonial subjects rising up to reclaim power after centuries of oppression. He even waded into the tumultuous waters of Jamaican domestic politics with "Ambushed in the Night" a song about his failed assassination attempt in which Marely strikes a defiant tone and expresses his belief that his life was spared thanks to divine intervention. This sent a clear message to Marley's fans that "Bob was going for broke, openly lending his strenuous support to the struggle for a truly free and independent Jamaica—a struggle which could very well end with the installation of a Black, Marxist government in a country that had long been dominated by right-wing colonialist white regimes" (White 2006, 303).

Bob Marley, Legend

Marley had played in the United States sporadically to this point, but he embarked on his first major US stadium tour in 1980. The tour received enormous media buzz, and the stage was set for Marley to become a superstar. Efforts had even been made to get the band significant coverage in Black publications for the first time in Marley's career, in an attempt to expand his appeal beyond his primarily white American rock audience (White 2006, 310). But it was not to be. Marley collapsed while jogging in Central Park, before playing a sold-out show at Madison Square Garden, and had to cut the tour short to undergo cancer treatment. Less than eight months later, he was dead at thirty-six years old.

The image that we have of Marley today was mostly constructed after his death, without the input of Marely himself. In the decades after his death, Marley has been slowly transformed from a militant, cannabis-smoking, Black revolutionary, to a pseudo-Christian mystic, championing a milquetoast vison of peace and racial harmony (Stephens 1998). This process of reimagining Marley began in earnest with the issuing of his greatest-hits album *Legend* in 1984. *Legend* is the album that made Marley a household name. It is by far the best-selling reggae album of all-time, with over 15 million copies sold in the United States, and more than 33 million sold globally (Haughton 2022). It is consistently rated as one of the "greatest albums of all time" by *Rolling Stone,* coming in at 48 on their 2020 revised list (Rolling Stone 2020). As of July 2023 it had spent a total of 792 nonconsecutive weeks on the US *Billboard* 200 albums chart—the second longest run in history, behind only Pink Floyd's *Dark Side of the Moon* (Young 2023).

Dave Robinson, who helped produce *Legend,* was open about the fact that he fully intended to use the album to soften Marley's image, in the hopes of garnering more mass-market appeal. This is something that many record executives had been pining for since the beginning. Danny Sims, Marley's manager, once told reporters, "I discouraged Bob from doing revolutionary stuff. I'm a commercial guy. I want to sell songs to thirteen-year-old girls, not to guys throwing spears" (as quoted in White 2006, 378). Yet Marley had largely resisted these efforts while he was alive. It goes too far to say that the softer, more commercial friendly music that the Wailers produced was not authentic to Marley, as some have suggested (Alleyne 1994). Marley wrote love songs throughout his career, and they appear on all the Wailers' albums. But, championing these softer songs, while simultaneously downplaying the more revolutionary aspects of Marley's music, offers a distorted image of him—one that primarily serves the evolving post-racial fantasies of Marley's growing white American fan base.

Robinson's market research indicated that "a lot of what people didn't like about Bob Marley was the threatening aspects of him, the revolutionary side" (Stephens 1998, 145). He sought to create an album that offered a more peaceful, family-friendly image of Marley. The word "reggae" was purposefully excluded from the album, as well as any obvious references to cannabis use. Robinson mostly ignored Marley's more politically explosive hits, in favor of love songs like "Is this Love," "No Woman No Cry," "Could You Be Loved," "Waiting in Vain," and "Satisfy My Soul." Bob Marley and the Wailers produced eleven albums for Island Records during the 1970s. Yet, *Legend* borrows overwhelmingly from just two— *Exodus* and *Kaya*. Half of the fourteen songs included on *Legend* were drawn from these two, somewhat aberrational, albums. Both "I Shot the Sheriff" and "Get Up Stand Up" were included, likely because those hits were so massive, they could not be avoided.[3] But nothing else from *Burnin'* appeared on this "greatest hits" album, and the band's most hard-hitting songs like "Burnin' and Lootin'," "Concrete Jungle," "War," and "Zimbabwe" were all left out. Indeed, not a single song from *Survival,* Marley's most revolutionary album, made the cut.

The album art was similarly designed to present Marley in a softer light. The cover includes a close-up picture of a contemplative Marley in a blue dress shirt. Instead of militant photos of Marley and his band mates smoking giant joints of cannabis, the album includes pictures of Marley smiling and playing with children. Most of these images came from a single photo shoot taken in London in 1977. These photos were not published until after Marley's death, in large part because the record company was concerned that they would have conflicted with the militant image of Marley that they were promoting at the time (Boot and Salewicz 1995, 197).

During the 1990s, Marley's image was further aided by the whitening of the cannabis space. His cannabis use, which was perceived as dangerous and revolutionary during the 1970s, now had the opposite effect, making him appear peaceful and relatively harmless. This has aided the Black artists who followed in his wake, most notably Calvin Broadus Jr., better known as "Snoop Dogg." Broadus connected so strongly with Marley, that he even briefly changed his name to "Snoop Lion" in honor of the singer (Magary 2012). Broadus first broke onto the music scene with hardcore gangster rap hits like "Murder Was the Case," which terrified white people (Baker 2018, 123–36). But he has been able to rehabilitate his image and gain mass appeal in part *because* of his association with cannabis. As Broadus himself once observed, "So what if I'm smokin' weed onstage and doing what I gotta do? It's not me shooting nobody, stabbing nobody, killing nobody. It's a peaceful gesture, and they have to respect that and appreciate that" (as quoted in McLeod 2022).

If anyone could resist this crude process of commodification, it should have been Marley. Everything about him—his Rastafarian religious beliefs, his Jamaican Patois, his revolutionary politics, his conspicuous consumption of "ganja," even his iconic dreadlocked mane—is tied up with his radical political beliefs as well as his racial identity. And yet, Marley's Blackness was rendered less meaningful by the unrelenting churn of the American capitalist system, as his more radical message of Black liberation was exchanged for platitudes about peace and racial harmony. This parallels changes in the perception of cannabis during this period as well. Cannabis has transitioned from being an exoticized, but revolutionary symbol, to a more buttoned-down, family friendly, activity with mass-market appeal. This transition has proved extremely lucrative for people like Broadus and to the beneficiaries of the Marley estate. But it has come at the cost of all but the most banal, self-serving, racial narratives, severely limiting its potential for delivering progressive social change.

Where Do We Go from Here?

> There was a fantastic universal sense that whatever we were doing was right, that we were winning. . . . Our energy would simply prevail. There was no point in fighting—on our side or theirs. We had all the momentum; we were riding the crest of a high and beautiful wave . . . less than five years later, you can go up on a steep hill in Las Vegas and look West, and with the right kind of eyes can almost see the high-water mark—that place where the wave finally broke and rolled back.
> —Hunter S. Thompson, *Fear and Loathing in Las Vegas* (1971, 68)

As I write these words, the cannabis reform movement is at a bit of a crossroads. Legalizing cannabis, hard as it was, seems, in retrospect, to have been the easy part. Making sure that the benefits of this new industry are distributed equitably is a more difficult task. These challenges are not unique to cannabis reform. The civil rights movement found itself in a similar situation following the historic passage of the Civil Rights and Voting Rights acts. In *Where Do We Go from Here,* Martin Luther King Jr. celebrates these achievements, but laments that they will not bring about true equality without further reforms. He writes that ending Jim Crow segregation is an extremely important, but largely symbolic step. Making sure that Black Americans are truly equal will require investing resources into communities that have been scarred by centuries of systemic racial discrimination. According to him, "a society that has done something special *against* the Negro for hundreds of years must now do something special *for* him, in order to equip him to compete on a just and equal basis" (King 1968, 95).

This is the bind that the cannabis reform movement finds itself in today. It should be clear by this point that allowing corporate cannabis to develop unchecked will not result in an equitable cannabis industry. It should also be clear that the proceeds from this industry *could* be used for more equitable purposes if we so desire. As King reminds us, "The poor can stop being poor if the rich are willing to become even richer at a slower rate" (King 1968, 6). If we are serious about using cannabis reform to advance racial justice though, corporations will have to accept smaller profits, and state governments may have to accept less tax revenue. Yet, thanks in part to the persistent neoliberal fantasy that unbridled free market capitalism is synonymous with freedom, Americans have historically been hostile to these types of redistributive economic policies—especially when people of color are the perceived beneficiaries. King acknowledges that "the great majority of Americans . . . are uneasy with injustice but unwilling to pay a significant price to eradicate it" (1968, 12).

There are no easy solutions to these problems, but we can start by putting racial equity at the center of our efforts to legalize cannabis. One of the saddest aspects of cannabis legalization is the missed opportunity to foreground equity in early cannabis legalization states like Washington, Colorado, Oregon, and California. Activists in these states are working hard to retroactively add social equity components to their cannabis legalization regimes, but as we saw in chapter 4, there are powerful groups, with a strong financial interest in preserving the status quo arrayed against them. The cannabis reform movement does seem to have taken these lessons to heart, however belatedly. Illinois was the eleventh state to legalize cannabis, but the first to make social equity a central part of these efforts. As we saw in chapter 3, the results have not lived up to the promises in that state, but the fact that equity is enshrined in law makes the job of activists there much easier. Illinois' missteps can also serve as a useful lesson for the states that follow it. New York, for example, just recently passed a cannabis legalization bill that addresses some of the problems with Illinois' social equity system. Many social justice–oriented cannabis activists are excited about its potential (Finberg, Menkes, and Wright 2022).

There are a number of ways to approach the task of building a more equitable cannabis industry. Some point to the need for more organized labor, which can hold corporations accountable and make sure that workers earn an equitable share of the profits (Marcus 2019). Others argue for the need to appeal to consumers and ask them to vote with their pocketbooks by patronizing minority-owned cannabis businesses and boycotting large multistate operators (Clark 2021). These are helpful solutions, but there is no path toward true equity that does not involve a significant role for the state as well. As this book has demonstrated, if left to its own devices, unbridled free market capitalism will only entrench inequality. The only force strong enough to counteract this is the government.

In the rare occasions when the US government has made efforts to regulate our capitalist economic system and redistribute resources more equitably, it has been remarkably successful. The Freedmen's Bureau was never funded adequately and was dismantled after only seven years of operations. Yet as W.E.B. Du Bois once wrote, "it was the most extraordinary and far-reaching institution of social uplift that America has ever attempted" (1935, 219) even though it, "was but a small and imperfect part of what it might have done if it had been made a permanent institution, given ample funds for operating schools and purchasing land, and if it had been gradually manned by trained civilian administrators" (230). There are clear parallels between the economic promises that the Freedmen's Bureau made to newly freed slaves, and the potential of legal cannabis. Hopefully, we will not look back on cannabis legalization a century from now with the same sense of what might have been.

Notes

Introduction

1. Law and society scholars have, for example, found law in popular films like *The Godfather* (Papke 1996), television crime dramas (Rapping 2003), late night television jokes (Haltom and McCann 2004), images of pregnant celebrities (Cramer 2016), and even the spy novels of William F. Buckley Jr. (Dudas 2017, 40–66).

2. Neoliberalism is an economic system that seeks to promote growth by encouraging the development of free markets and discouraging government regulation of business. In this book, however, I am less concerned with neoliberalism as formal economic policy, and more interested in how these ideas are reinforced through powerful political, moral, and cultural logics—what Wendy Brown refers to as "neoliberal political rationality" (2003). As Stephanie Mudge has argued, the basic tenants of neoliberalism, which hold that unfettered economic markets are the best way to distribute scarce resources and maintain a free society, have become so ingrained in Western culture since at least the 1980s, that they have acquired quasi-religious significance (2008). In this way neoliberalism's impact extends beyond government policy, shaping individual behavior by creating a society where materialism, conspicuous consumption, and the maximization of profits are seen as the hallmarks of good citizenship.

3. Similar arrest data for Latinos is unavailable because the FBI Uniform Crime Report does not disaggregate based on ethnicity. This could also have the effect of artificially lowering the perceived disparity in black/white arrest rates.

4. Colorado, which had the smallest racial disparity in cannabis arrests, still arrested Black people for cannabis possession at a rate 1.5 times higher than whites. Il-

linois had the highest disparity in arrests among legal states during this time period, arresting Black people for cannabis possession at a rate 7.5 times higher than whites, an increase of 118 percent since cannabis was legalized in the state (ACLU 2020, 32-33).

5. States that legalize cannabis have tended to see precipitous declines in cannabis arrest rates. One study found that states that legalized cannabis between 2010 and 2018 saw their cannabis arrest rates drop from 173.7 per 100,000 to 24.5 per 100,000 (ACLU 2020, 25).

6. Most of my interviewees reported being affiliated with multiple cannabis activist organizations. Thirteen identified as members of NORML's national organization, fifteen with various local chapters of NORML, two with DPA, two with MPP, ten with ASA, five with Students for Sensible Drug Policy (SSDP), three with Patients out of Time (POT), three with Law Enforcement Against Prohibition (LEAP), four with the National Cannabis Industry Association (NCIA), five with the Cannabis Alliance, and twenty-six were affiliated with "other" local cannabis organizations.

7. In order to ensure a diverse pool of interviewees, I solicited interviewees from a number of pro-cannabis organizations that focus specifically on communities of color, such as the Minority Cannabis Business Association, the Black Cannabis Commission, Cannabis Equity Illinois, and Minorities for Medical Marijuana.

8. Six identified as Black, one as Latino, two as Asian American or Pacific Islander, and one as Native American.

9. Thirteen lived in Washington at the time of our interview, eight in California, three in Illinois, two each from Nevada, Michigan, and Florida, one each from Oregon, Colorado, Minnesota, Ohio, Massachusetts, New York, and Washington, DC. Ten of my interviewees lived in Washington, DC, and participated mostly in cannabis activism at the federal level. Two of my interviewees were Canadian cannabis activists.

Chapter 1

1. When possible, I tried to speak directly with people who participated in these events or were impacted by these changes, including those who worked in the illicit or medical cannabis industry, engaged in cannabis activism, or both. I supplemented these interviews with textual analysis of relevant historical documents, and a careful reading of secondary source materials.

2. THC, or delta-9-tetrahydrocannabinol, is one of over 100 cannabinoids found in the cannabis plant. It is thought to be the primary psychoactive ingredient in cannabis.

3. Sometimes spelled "marihuana," especially in older publications.

4. The Emerald Triangle refers to three counties in California's north coast

(Humboldt, Mendocino, and Trinity) that collectively produce the most cannabis in the United States. The remote region is ideal for producing cannabis due to its mild climate and remoteness. It is often compared favorably to California's Napa Valley, which is famous for producing fine wines.

5. Thomas Jefferson famously said that farmers were "the chosen people of god" and a "deposit for substantial and genuine virtue" (Jefferson 1785, 259). In the frontier narrative the farmer is usually the one who brings civilization to the "howling wilderness." Through hard work and dedication, he is able to tame the wild lands and make productive use of them (Crevecoeur 1782). This was often contrasted with groups like American Indians, who were deemed unworthy of citizenship because they were not thought to engage in agriculture.

6. Schedule I substances are drugs that the federal government deems have "a high potential for abuse" and "no medicinal value." Possession or sale of these substances is typically punished severely by the federal government, and their use for medical or research purposes is tightly restricted. Along with cannabis, the federal government also lists heroin, LSD, ecstasy, methaqualone (Quaaludes), and peyote as Schedule I (Drug Enforcement Agency 2020a).

7. Studies measuring the effectiveness of these campaigns have found that they had little impact on the demand for drugs (West and O'Neal 2004; Hornik et al. 2008).

8. Rathbun was once arrested with two and a half pounds of cannabis in her possession. In response, she defiantly proclaimed to the media that "if the narcs think I'm going to stop baking pot brownies form my kids with AIDS, they can go fuck themselves in Macy's window!" (as quoted in Hecht 2014, 49). All chargers against her were eventually dropped.

Chapter 2

1. In 1992 Bill Clinton famously declared that he had tried cannabis as a Rhodes Scholar at Oxford, but that he "didn't inhale." The comment became fodder for late-night comedians, but Clinton's cagey response was probably smart politics. Just five years earlier Douglas Ginsberg had been forced to withdraw his nomination to the US Supreme Court after it was revealed that he had smoked cannabis as an assistant professor at Harvard. As recently as 2005, George W. Bush, who had been open about his past struggles with alcohol and cocaine, refused to answer "the marijuana question." Today, political candidates frequently admit to having smoked cannabis without suffering negative consequences, but they are usually still careful to characterized this use as a harmless youthful experiment.

2. Boehner was a staunch opponent of cannabis throughout his political career, but says that he has since "evolved" on the issue. He currently works as a lobbyist for the cannabis industry and has invested in several cannabis-related business ventures (Williamson 2019).

3. As of this writing cannabis has been legalized for adult use in: Washington (2012), Colorado (2012), Oregon (2014), Alaska (2014), Washington, DC (2014), California (2016), Nevada (2016), Maine (2016), Massachusetts (2016), Vermont (2018), Michigan (2018), Illinois (2019), Arizona (2020), Montana (2021), New Jersey (2021), Connecticut (2021), New Mexico (2021), New York (2021), Virginia (2021), Rhode Island (2022), Missouri (2022), Maryland (2023), Delaware (2023), Minnesota (2023), and Ohio (2023).

4. The Marijuana Opportunity Reinvestment and Expungement Act (MORE Act), which would legalize cannabis at the federal level, was approved by the House of Representatives in both 2019 and 2021, before dying in the Senate.

5. American popular culture is replete with examples of heroic outlaw characters like these, from Bonnie and Clyde, to the vigilante cowboys of the Wild West, to the Godfather. Despite their outlaw status, these figures contain many admirable qualities. They may be outlaws, but they are outlaws who embody a culture of rugged individualisms and self-reliance that has long been celebrated as a cornerstone of American identity (Engel 1984, 558–62; Bellah et al. 1985).

6. This figure was calculated by the author by taking the number of pages per issue dedicated exclusively to advertisements and dividing that by the total number of pages in the issue.

7. Weedmaps is a California tech company that aggregates information about all adult use and medical cannabis dispensaries, and then provides that information to consumers. The company was founded in 2008, before any state had legalized cannabis, and was particularly helpful for consumers trying to navigate the unregulated medical cannabis market.

8. Frames are thematic "interpretive packages" that help individuals to make sense of the world (Gamson and Modigliani 1989, 2).

9. The *Marijuana Business Daily* survey likely overestimated the amount of minority ownership in the cannabis industry for a variety of reasons. First, it allowed people who are biracial to identify as more than one race. This could result in a double count of many minority respondents. The survey also includes "ancillary businesses" such as marketing, security, and transportation companies as part of the cannabis industry. These "non plant touching" businesses are not as tightly regulated or as lucrative, and are usually excluded from state-level data on the cannabis industry. The survey also counted anyone with an ownership stake as an "owner" even though most minority cannabis business owners do not have a controlling stake in their business (Quinton 2021). The state-level data is much better in these regards, as they count only cannabis business license holders. However, in both Nevada and Michigan a significant percentage of respondents refused to disclose their racial identity, potentially skewing the results. These people are included as "other" in the dataset.

Chapter 3

1. The estimated startup cost of a cannabis business range anywhere from $150,000 at the low end, to $2 million or more in some states. This is significantly more than the startup cost of most new business ventures (Kovacevich 2019).

2. In Illinois for example, those applying for a craft growing license, which is seen as the best opportunity for equity applicants looking to break into the industry, are asked to submit hundreds of pages of written material. Successful applicants must write up to 65 pages about their security plan, 50 pages on their cultivation plan, up to 15 pages on the suitability of their employee training program, up to 55 pages on their product safety and labeling plan, and up to 60 pages on their business plan, and an unlimited number of pages on the suitability of their proposed facility (Illinois Department of Agriculture 2020).

3. At the time of this writing only a handful of legal cannabis states still had no mechanism that allowed for the expungement of low-level cannabis offenses. Those states include: Alaska, Arizona, Virginia, and Maine (Hartman 2020).

4. Qualified equity applicants in Illinois receive 50 points (out of a possible total of 250) for dispensary license applications and receive 200 points (out of possible total 1,000) for craft grower, infuser, or transporter license applications (Illinois Department of Commerce and Economic Opportunity 2021)

5. At the time of this writing, six states provide qualified equity applicants with technical assistance, reduced application fees, or other licensing preferences (Massachusetts, Michigan, Illinois, Washington, New York, and New Jersey). Illinois and New York go further by providing low-interest loans to qualified applicants, and by investing a significant portion of their cannabis tax receipts back into the communities most harmed by the War on Drugs (Minority Cannabis Business Association 2022).

6. The licensing process was delayed, first because of the COVID-19 pandemic, and then because the state botched the initial round of licensing, resulting in most of the cannabis business licenses being awarded to large multistate operators backed by wealthy, politically connected, white investors. The ensuing outrage forced lawmakers to revise the equity application process and generated a slew of lawsuits from angry applicants, adding further delays (Meadows 2020).

7. Under Illinois law an area is considered a "Disproportionately Impacted Area" (DIA) if: (1) it has a poverty rate of at least 20 percent; (2) at least 75 percent of the children in that area participate in the federal free lunch program; (3) at least 20 percent of the households in the area receive assistance under the Supplemental Nutrition Assistance Program; or (4) it has an average unemployment rate that is more than 120 percent of the national average (Cannabis Regulation and Tax Act 2019).

8. There are many problems with the illicit cannabis industry that could be ad-

dressed with effective government regulations. Regulations could, for example, be used to prevent illicit cannabis farms from causing ecological and environmental damage (Miller 2018) or to protect illicit cannabis workers from financial exploitation and sexual assault (Walter 2016).

Chapter 4

1. At the time of this writing only three states, Nebraska, Idaho, and Kansas, prohibit all medical cannabis use. Nine other states allow nonintoxicating cannabinoids like CBD to be used for medical purposes, but prohibit cannabis products, which contain THC: Wyoming, Iowa, Wisconsin, Indiana, Tennessee, Texas, North Carolina, South Carolina, and Georgia. The remaining 38 states have comprehensive medical cannabis programs (National Conference of State Legislatures, 2023).

2. At the time of this writing a few states still have residency requirements on the books, but most contain loopholes that can be easily exploited. New Jersey, for example, requires only that applicants have "at least one owner" who has resided in the state for two years prior to the date of application. In contrast Washington and Alaska both stipulate that a nonresident "may not own any stake" in a cannabis business (Rodriguez, Sava, and Jordan 2022).

Conclusion

1. For an excellent overview of the source material, veracity, and basic tenants of the Rastafarian religion see White 1983, 1–28.

2. The lyrics of the song include the lines "Every time I plant a seed/ He said, 'kill it before it grow'" which is usually interpreted as a reference to growing cannabis, but may also have been an allusion to Marley's moral opposition to birth control (Uitti 2022).

3. "I Shot the Sheriff," in particular, gained widespread acclaim after Eric Clapton covered it in 1974. His cover became a bigger hit than the original, and garnered widespread radio airplay during the 1970s.

Works Cited

ACLU. 2020. "A Tale of Two Countries: Racially Targeted Arrests in the Era of Marijuana Reform." Accessed May 23, 2020. https://www.aclu.org/sites/default/files/field_document/042020-marijuanareport.pdf.

———. 2022. "ACLU Criminal Law Reform Project." Accessed October 4, 2022. https://www.aclu.org/other/aclu-criminal-law-reform-project.

Alinsky, Saul. 1971. *Rules for Radicals: A Practical Primer for Realistic Radicals*. New York: Random House.

Allen, Garry. 2022. "Can Independent Stores Compete with MSOs in the Adult-Use Markets?" *mg Magazine*, May 18. Accessed June 29, 2022. https://mgmagazine.com/business/retail-merchandise/can-independent-stores-compete-with-msos-in-adult-use-markets/.

Alleyne, Mike. 1994. "Positive Vibration?: Capitalist Textual Hegemony and Bob Marley." *Caribbean Studies* 27 (3–4): 224–41.

Allport, Gordon W. 1954. *The Nature of Prejudice*. New York: Doubleday.

Anderson, Septembre. 2015. "Oppressive Office Dress Codes Need to Go." *Vice*, July 7. Accessed August 12, 2020. https://www.vice.com/en_us/article/8gkgy4/its-time-to-rethink-eurocentric-office-dress-codes.

Avetisian, Jake, and Ross Stone. 2022. "'Higher' Education: Trends and Issues in University Cannabis Programing." *Council for Federal Cannabis Regulation*, August. Accessed May 2, 2023. https://admin.uscfcr.org/wp-content/uploads/2022/09/CFCR_Higher-Education_-Evaluating-Trends-in-Cannabis-Educational-Programming-2.pdf.

Aviram, Hadar. 2015. *Cheap on Crime: Recession-Era Politics and the Transformation of American Punishment*. Berkeley: University of California Press.

Baker, Al, David Goodman, and Benjamin Mueller. 2015. "Beyond the Chokehold: The Path to Eric Garner's Death." *New York Times*. Accessed July 16,

2021. https://www.nytimes.com/2015/06/14/nyregion/eric-garner-police-choke-hold-staten-island.html.

Baker, Soren. 2018. *The History of Gangster Rap: From Schooly D to Kendrick Lamar, The Rise of a Great American Art Form*. New York: Abrams Image.

Barcott, Bruce. 2017. *Marijuana Goes Main Street*. New York: Time Books.

Barcott, Bruce, Beau Whitney, and Janessa Bailey. 2021. "Jobs Report 2021: The US Cannabis Industry Now Supports 321,000 Full-Time Jobs." *Leafly*. Accessed August 1, 2021. https://leafly-cms-production.imgix.net/wp-content/uploads/2021/02/13180206/Leafly-JobsReport, 2021-v14.pdf.

Baum, Dan. 1996. *Smoke and Mirrors: The War on Drugs and the Politics of Failure*. Boston: Little Brown.

Becker, Gary. 1957. *The Economics of Discrimination*. Chicago: University of Chicago Press.

Bell, Derek. 1992. *Faces at the Bottom of the Well: The Permanence of Racism*. New York: Basic Books.

Bellah, Robert, Richard Madsen, William Sullivan, Ann Swidler, and Steven Tipton. 1985. *Habits of the Heart: Individualism and Commitment in American Life*. Berkeley: University of California Press.

Bender, Steven. 2016. "The Color of Cannabis: Race and Cannabis." *UC Davis Law Review* 50:689–706.

Benford, Robert D., and David Snow. 2000. "Framing Processes and Social Movements: An Overview and Assessment." *Annual Review of Sociology* 26:611–39.

Berman, Douglas. 2018. "Leveraging Marijuana Reforms to Enhance Expungement Practices." *Federal Sentencing Reporter* 30 (4–5): 305–16.

Bernstein, Jen. 2014. "The Booming Business of Buds." *High Times*, October, 46–54.

Berrey, Ellen. 2015. *The Enigma of Diversity: The Language of Race and the Limits of Racial Justice*. Chicago: University of Chicago Press.

Bhutta, Neil, Andrew Chang, Lisa Dettling, and Joanne Hsu. 2020. "Disparities in Wealth by Race and Ethnicity in the 2019 Survey of Consumer Finances." *Federal Reserve Notes*. Accessed April 7, 2021. https://www.federalreserve.gov/econres/notes/feds-notes/disparities-in-wealth-by-race-and-ethnicity-in-the-2019-survey-of-consumer-finances-20200928.htm.

Bonnie, Richard, and Charles Whitebread. 1974. *The Marijuana Conviction: A History of Marijuana Prohibition in the United States*. Charlottesville: University Press of Virginia.

Boot, Adrian, and Chris Salewicz. 1995. *Bob Marley: Songs of Freedom*. New York: Vintage Books.

Booth, Martin. 2003. *Cannabis: A History*. London: Bantam Books.

Brady, Emily. 2013. *Humboldt: Life on America's Marijuana Frontier*. London: Scribe Books.

Brenan, Megan. 2020. "Support for Legal Marijuana Inches Up to New High of

68%" *Gallup*. Accessed October 4, 2022. https://news.gallup.com/poll/323582/support-legal-marijuana-inches-new-high.aspx.

Brewers Association. 2021. "National Beer Sales and Production Data." Accessed January 5, 2021. https://www.brewersassociation.org/statistics-and-data/national-beer-stats/.

Bricken, Hilary. 2018. "The Good, the Bad, and the Ugly: Social Equity Cannabis in Los Angeles." *Above the Law*. Accessed July 16, 2021. https://abovethelaw.com/2018/08/the-good-the-bad-and-the-ugly-social-equity-cannabis-in-los-angeles/.

Bridges, Khiara. 2017. *The Poverty of Privacy Rights*. Stanford, CA: Stanford University Press.

Brown, Wendy. 2003. "Neo-Liberalism and the End of Liberal Democracy." *Theory and Event* 7 (1): 15–18.

Butler, George. 1977. "Drug Store Cowboys." *High Times*, February, 76–78, 96.

Calavita, Kitty. 2016. *Invitation to Law and Society: An Introduction to the Study of Real Law*. 2nd ed. Chicago: University of Chicago Press.

California Department of Cannabis Control. 2022. "Where Cannabis Businesses Are Allowed." Accessed September 5, 2022. https://cannabis.ca.gov/cannabis-laws/where-cannabis-businesses-are-allowed/.

Campos Isaac. 2018. "Mexicans and the Origins of Marijuana Prohibition in the United States: A Reassessment." *Social History of Alcohol and Drugs* 32:6–37.

Carmichael, Stokely. 1966. "What We Want." *New York Review of Books*, September 22. https://www.nybooks.com/articles/1966/09/22/what-we-want/.

Chander, Raj. 2022. "Will Social Equity in Illinois Live Up to the Hype?" *Leafly*. Accessed September 19, 2022. https://www.leafly.com/news/industry/will-social-equity-in-illinois-live-up-to-the-hype.

Chapkis, Wendy, and Richard J. Webb. 2008. *Dying to Get High: Cannabis as Medicine*. New York: New York University Press.

Chemerinsky, Erwin, Jolene Forman, Allen Hopper, and Sam Kamin. 2015. "Cooperative Federalism and Marijuana Regulation." *UCLA Law Review* 62:74–122.

Ciaramella, C. J. 2019. "The Future of Marijuana Expungement Is Automatic." Accessed September 16, 2022. https://reason.com/2019/04/20/the-future-of-marijuana-expungements-is-automation/.

Cioffi, Joseph, Nicole Serratore, and Anna Pinna. 2021. "State Residency Rules Up in Smoke as Cannabis Industry Grows." *Reuters*. Accessed June 21, 2022. https://www.reuters.com/legal/litigation/state-residency-rules-up-smoke-cannabis-industry-grows-2021-11-05/.

Clark, Kevin L. 2021. "10 Black-Owned Cannabis Brands You Can Support" *Ebony*. Accessed November 14, 2022. https://www.ebony.com/black-august-black-owned-cannabis-brands-to-support/.

Congressional Research Service. 2020. "Real Wage Trends, 1979 to 2019." Accessed July 29, 2021. https://fas.org/sgp/crs/misc/R45090.pdf.

Corva, Dominic, and Josha S. Meisel. 2022. "Introduction to Post-Prohibition."

In *The Routledge Handbook of Post-Prohibition Cannabis Studies*, ed. Dominic Corva and Joshua Meisel, 1–22. New York: Routledge.

Coughlin-Bogue, Tobias. 2016. "The Word 'Marijuana' Versus the Word 'Cannabis': And Why I'm Going to Stop Using the Former in this Column." *The Stranger*. Accessed October 29, 2020. https://www.thestranger.com/ news/2016/04/13/23948555/the-word-marijuana-versus-the-word-cannabis.

Courtwright, David. 2001. *Forces of Habit: Drugs and the Making of the Modern World*. Cambridge, MA: Harvard University Press.

Cover, Robert M. 1986. "Violence and the Word." *Yale Law Journal* 95:1601–29.

Cramer, Renee. 2016. *Pregnant with the Stars: Watching and Wanting the Celebrity Baby Bump*. Palo Alto, CA: Stanford University Press.

Crenshaw, Kimberle. 1988. "Race, Reform, and Retrenchment: Transformation and Legitimation in Antidiscrimination Law." *Harvard Law Review* 101 (7): 1331–87.

Crevecoeur, Hector St. Jean. 1782. "Letter from an American Farmer." In *Early American Writing*, ed Giles Gunn, 472–79. London: Penguin Books.

Criminal Justice Policy Foundation. 2019. "Cannabis Policy (Cannabis)." Accessed July 25, 2019. https://www.cjpf.org/cannabis.

Crocq, Marc-Antoine. 2020. "History of Cannabis and the Endocannabinoid System." *Dialogues in Clinical Neuroscience* 22 (3): 223–28.

Davis, Angela. 2019. "Reimagining Prosecution: A Growing Progressive Movement." *UCLA Criminal Justice Law Review* 3 (1): 1–27

Demko, Paul, and Alexander Nieves. 2020. "The Pandemic Is Eating Away at the Illicit Marijuana Market." *Politico*, August 2. Accessed April 6, 2021. https:// www.politico.com/news/2020/08/02/pandemic-illicit-marijuana-market-390175.

Donnan, Jennifer, Omar Shogan, Lisa Bishop, Michelle Swab, and Maisam Najafizada. 2022. "Characteristics that Influence Purchase Choice for Cannabis Products: A Systematic Review." *Journal of Cannabis Research* 4 (9). https://doi. org/10.1186/s42238-022-00117-0.

Drug Enforcement Agency. 2020a. "Drug Scheduling." Accessed May 23, 2020. https://www.dea.gov/drug-scheduling.

———. 2020b. "National Drug Threat Assessment." Accessed September 19, 2020. https://www.dea.gov/sites/default/files/2021-02/DIR-008-21%202020%20National%20 Drug%20Threat%20Assessment_WEB.pdf.

Drug Policy Alliance. 2022. "Criminal Justice Reform." Accessed July 25, 2019. http://www.drugpolicy.org/issues/criminal-justice-reform.

Du Bois, W. E. B. 1935. *Black Reconstruction in America: 1860–1880*. New York: Free Press.

Dudas, Jeffrey. 2017. *Raised Right: Fatherhood in Modern American Conservatism*. Stanford, CA: Stanford University Press.

Dudas, Jeffrey, Johnathon Goldberg-Hiller, and Michael McCann. 2015. "The Past, Present, and Future of Rights Scholarship." In *The Handbooilk of Law and Society*, ed. Austin Sarat and Patricia Ewick, 367–81. Hoboken, NJ: Wiley-Blackwell.

Eagles, Charles W. 2000. "Toward New Histories of the Civil Rights Era." *Journal of Southern History* 66 (4): 815–48.

Engel, David M. 1984. "The Oven Bird's Song: Insiders, Outsiders, and Personal Injuries in an American Community." *Law and Society Review.* 18 (4): 551–82.

Engel, David M., and Frank W. Munger. 2003. *Rights of Inclusion: Law and Identity in the Life Stories of Americans with Disabilities.* Chicago: University of Chicago Press.

Epstein, Richard. 1992. *Forbidden Grounds: The Case Against Employment Discrimination Laws.* Cambridge, MA: Harvard University Press.

Ewick, Patricia, and Susan S. Silbey. 1998. *The Common Place of Law: Stories from Everyday Life.* Chicago: University of Chicago Press.

Felson, Jacob, Amy Adamczyk, and Christopher Thomas. 2019. "How and Why Have Attitudes about Cannabis Legalization Changed So Much? *Social Science Research* 78:12–27.

Fertig, Natalie. 2019. "How Legal Marijuana Is Helping the Black Market." *Politico*, July 21. Accessed April 6, 2021. https://www.politico.com/magazine/story/2019/07/21/legal-marijuana-black-market-227414/.

———. 2020. "Local Rule Is Undermining Massachusetts' Attempt to Create Equity in the Cannabis Industry." *Politico*, March 6. Accessed April 7, 2021. https://www.politico.com/news/2020/03/06/local-rule-is-undermining-massachusetts-attempt-to-create-equity-in-the-cannabis-industry-122655.

Finberg, Abraham, Simon Menkes, and Rachel Wright. 2022. "The Great Social Experiment: Social Equity in New York." *Cannabis Industry Journal*, March 18. Accessed November 14, 2022. https://cannabisindustryjournal.com/feature_article/the-great-social-experiment-social-equity-in-new-york/.

Foucault, Michel. 1978. *Discipline and Punish: The Birth of the Prison.* New York: Pantheon Books.

Fourcher, Mike. 2021. "Leaked Illinois State Report Shows Black and Latinos Owned Less Than 2% of Dispensaries Last June." *Grown In*, February 22. Accessed July 16, 2021. https://grownin.com/2021/02/22/leaked-illinois-state-report-shows-black-and-latinos-owned-less-than-2-of-dispensaries-last-june/.

Franke, Katherine. 2015. *Wedlocked: The Perils of Marriage Equality.* New York: New York University Press.

Galanter, Marc. 1974. "Why the 'Haves' Come Out Ahead: Speculations on the Limits of Legal Change." *Law and Society Review* 9 (1): 95–160.

Gamson, William A., and Andre Modigliani. 1989. "Media Discourse and Public Opinion on Nuclear Power: A Constructionist Approach." *American Journal of Sociology* 95 (1): 1–37.

Garland, David. 1990. *Punishment and Modern Society: A Study in Social Theory.* Chicago: University of Chicago Press.

Garriott, William. 2020. "Change is in the Air: The Smell of Marijuana, after Legalization." *Law and Social Inquiry* 45:995–1026.

Gilliom, John. 2001. *Overseers of the Poor: Surveillance, Resistance, and the Limits of Privacy.* Chicago: University of Chicago Press.

Gilliom, John, and Torin Monahan. 2012. *SuperVision: An Introduction to the Surveillance Society.* Chicago: University of Chicago Press.

Glendon, Mary Ann. 1993. *Rights Talk: The Impoverishment of Political Discourse.* New York: Free Press.

Goldberg, Chad Alan. 2007. *Citizens and Paupers: Relief, Rights, and Race, from the Freedmen's Bureau to Workfare.* Chicago: University of Chicago Press.

Gottschalk, Marie. 2006. *The Prison and the Gallows: The Politics of Mass Incarceration in America.* New York: Cambridge University Press.

Hale, Grace Elizabeth. 2011. *A Nation of Outsiders: How the White Middle Class Fell in Love with Rebellion in Postwar America.* New York: Oxford University Press.

Hale, Robert L. 1923. "Coercion and Distribution in a Supposedly Non-Coercive State." *Political Science Quarterly* 38 (3): 470–94.

Hall, Jacquelyn Dowd. 2005. "The Long Civil Rights Movement and the Political Uses of the Past." *Journal of American History* 91 (4): 1233–63.

Haltom, William, and Michael McCann. 2004. *Distorting the Law: Politics, Media, and the Litigation Crisis.* Chicago: University of Chicago Press.

Hamilton, Jack. 2016. *Just Around Midnight: Rock and Roll and the Racial Imagination.* Cambridge, MA: Harvard University Press.

Hartman, Michael. 2020. "States Move to Clear Records of People with Previous Pot Convictions." *National Conference of State Legislatures.* Accessed September 16, 2022. https://www.ncsl.org/research/civil-and-criminal-justice/clearing-criminal-records-of-previous-marijuana-convictions-magazine2020.aspx.

Harris, Angela. 2021. "Racial Capitalism and the Law." In *Histories of Racial Capitalism*, ed. Destin Jenkins and Justin Leroy, vii–xx. New York: Columbia University Press.

Harris, Fredrick C. 2014. *The Price of the Ticket: Barack Obama and the Rise and Decline of Black Politics.* New York: Oxford University Press.

Haughton, G. 2022. "Marley, Wailers' 'Legend' Best-Selling Reggae Album." *Caribbean National Weekly*, January 13. Accessed August 2, 2023. https://www.caribbeannationalweekly.com/entertainment/marley-wailers-legend-best-selling-reggae-album/.

Hawkesworth, Mary. 2006. "Contending Conceptions of Science and Politics: Methodology and the Constitution of the Political." In *Interpretation and Method: Empirical Research Methods and the Interpretive Turn*, ed Dvora Yanow and Peregrine Schwartz-Shea, 27–49. London: M. E. Sharpe.

Hecht, Peter. 2014. *Weed Land: Inside America's Cannabis Epicenter and How Pot Went Legit.* Berkeley, CA: University of California Press.

Higginbotham, Evelyn Brooks. 1994. *Righteous Discontent: The Woman's Movement in the Black Baptist Church, 1880–1920.* Cambridge, MA: Harvard University Press.

Himmelstein, Jerome. 1983. *The Strange Career of Marihuana*. Westport, CT: Greenwood.

Hoban, Robert. 2021. "The Year of Cannabis Industry Consolidation." *Forbes*, March 22. Accessed July 16, 2021. https://www.forbes.com/sites/robertho-ban/2021/03/22/the-year-of-cannabis-industry-consolidation/?sh=6c91072e7715.

Holmes, Oliver Wendell, Jr. 1897. "The Path of the Law." *Harvard Law Review* 10 (8): 457–78.

Hornik, Robert, Lela Jacobsohn, Robert Orwin, Andrea Piesse, and Graham Kalton. 2008. "Effects of the National Youth Anti-Drug Media Campaigns on Youths." *American Journal of Public Health* 98 (12): 2229–36.

Illinois Department of Agriculture. 2020. "Cannabis Craft Grower Application and Exhibits." Accessed September 16, 2022. https://www2.illinois.gov/sites/agr/Plants/Documents/Craft%20Grower%20Application%20and%20Exhibits%20Form.pdf.

Illinois Department of Commerce and Economic Opportunity. 2021. "Illinois Adult-Use Cannabis Social Equity Program." Accessed July 16, 2021. https://www2.illinois.gov/dceo/CannabisEquity/Pages/default.aspx.

Jefferson, Thomas. 1785. "Notes on Virginia." In *The Life and Selected Writings of Thomas Jefferson*, ed. Adrienne Koch and William Peden, 173–268. New York: Random House.

Jenkins, Destin, and Justin Leroy. 2021. "The Old History of Capitalism." In *Histories of Racial Capitalism*, ed. Jenkins and Leroy, 1–26. New York: Columbia University Press.

Johnson, Emma. 2015. "Turning Green Into Gold: Pot Jobs Report." *High Times*, October, 58–64.

Johnson, Nick. 2017. *Grass Roots: A History of Cannabis in the American West*. Corvallis: Oregon State University Press.

———. 2019. "American Weed: A History of Cannabis Cultivation in the United States." *EchoGeo*, 48. https://doi.org/10.4000/echogeo.17650.

Jonnes, Jill. 1996 *Hep-Cats, Narcs and Pipe Dreams: A History of America's Romance with Illicit Drugs*. New York: Scribner.

Kary, Tiffany. 2021. "Lessons from California's Pot Industry Bailout." *Bloomberg*, June 21. Accessed July 16, 2021. https://www.bloomberg.com/news/articles/2021-06-21/lessons-from-california-s-pot-industry-bailout-cannabis-weekly.

Kaufman, Katie. 2022. "Changing the Face of the Stoner: Images of Race and Gender in Cannabis Legalization Campaigns in the United States." In *The Routledge Handbook of Post-Prohibition Cannabis Studies*, ed. Dominic Corva and Joshua Meisel, 314–22. New York: Routledge.

Kerouac, Jack. 1957. *On the Road*. New York: Viking Press.

Kilmer, Beau, and Robert J. MacCoun. 2017. "How Medical Marijuana Smoothed the Transition to Marijuana Legalization in the United States." *Annual Review of Law and Social Science* 13:181–202.

King, Martin Luther, Jr. 1963. "Letter from a Birmingham Jail." Accessed July 25,

2023. https://billofrightsinstitute.org/primary-sources/letter-from-birming-ham-jail.

———. 1968. *Where do We go From Here: Chaos or Community?* Boston: Beacon Street Press.

Kingdon, John. 1995. *Agenda, Alternative, and Public Policies.* 2nd ed. New York: HarperCollins.

Kinley, Dadriana. 2023. "Cannabis Administration & Opportunity Act Comments." Accessed 11-20-2023. https://nuproject.org/cannabis-administration-opportunity-act-comments/.

Koram, Kojo. 2022. "The Legalization of Cannabis and the Question of Reparations." *Journal of International Economic Law* 25 (2): 294–311.

Kornbluth, Jesse. 1978. "Poisonous Fallout from the War on Marijuana." *New York Times*, November 19.

Kovacevich, Nick. 2019. "The Hidden Cost of the Cannabis Business." *Forbes*, February 1. Accessed September 16, 2022. https://www.forbes.com/sites/nickkovacevich/2019/02/01/the-hidden-costs-of-the-cannabis-business/?sh=1f4f302f7da3.

Leachman, Gwendolyn. 2014. "From Protest to *Perry*: How Litigation Shaped the LGBT Movement's Agenda." *U.C. Davis Law Review* 47:1667–1751.

Lee, Martin A. 2012. *Smoke Signals: A Social History of Marijuana—Medical, Recreational, and Scientific.* New York: Scribner.

Lemmo, Robert. 1975. "Pot, Peasants, and Pancho Villa." *High Times*, Winter, 32–33, 36–37.

Lovell, George I. 2012. *This Is Not Civil Rights: Discovering Rights Talk in 1939 America.* Chicago: University of Chicago Press.

Magary, Drew. 2012. "The Lion Smokes Tonight." *GQ*, January. Accessed August 1, 2023. https://www.gq.com/story/snoop-lion-snoop-dogg-profile-gq-january-2013.

Mailer, Norman. (1957) 2007. "The White Negro: Superficial Reflections on the Hipster." *Dissent*, June 20. Accessed July 25, 2023. https://www.dissentmagazine.org/online_articles/the-white-negro-fall-1957/.

Manderson, Desmond. 1999. "Symbolism and Racism in Drug History and Policy." *Drug and Alcohol Review* 18 (2): 179–86.

Marcus, Josh. 2019. "Meet America's Most Powerful Cannabis Union." *Rolling Stone*, June 14. Accessed November 14, 2022. https://www.rollingstone.com/culture/culture-features/cannabis-weed-union-jobs-ufcw-846505/.

Marley Natural. 2014. "Big News: Privateer Holdings to Launch Marley Natural, World's 1st Global Cannabis Brand." Accessed November 20, 2023. https://www.bobmarley.com/marley-natural/.

Mattson, Kevin. 2002. "Civil Rights Made Harder." *Reviews in American History* 30 (4): 663–70.

Mayo-Adams, Erin. 2020. *Queer Alliances: How Power Shapes Political Movement Formation.* Stanford, CA: Stanford University Press.

McAdam, Doug. 1999. *Political Process and the Development of Black Insurgency, 1930–1970.* 2nd ed. Chicago: University of Chicago Press.

McCann, Michael. 1994. *Rights at Work: Pay Equity Reform and the Politics of Legal Mobilization.* Chicago: University of Chicago Press.

———. 1996. "Causal versus Constitutive *Explanations* (or, On the Difficulty of Being so Positive . . .)." *Law and Social Inquiry* 21:457–82.

———. 2020. *Union by Law: Filipino Labor Activists, Rights Radicalism, and Racial Capitalism.* Chicago: University of Chicago Press.

McCluney, Courtney, Kathrina Robotham, Serenity Lee, Richard Smith, and Myles Durkee. 2019. "The Cost of Code Switching." *Harvard Business Review*, November 15. Accessed July 28, 2021. https://hbr.org/2019/11/the-costs-of-codeswitching.

McCoppin, Robert. 2021. "Cannabis Industry in Illinois Sees Increased Minority Ownership—but Delayed Startups Say They May Have to Sell Out." *Chicago Tribune*, December 7. Accessed September 19, 2022. https://www.chicagotribune.com/marijuana/illinois/ct-illinois-marijuana-minority-owner-ship-20211207-gtosbd6pkvc7hgwvu3zpzftypi-story.html.

McLeod, Nia Simone. 2022. "Snoop Dogg Quotes to Remind You How to Stay Fly." *Everyday Power.* Accessed August 2, 2023. https://everydaypower.com/snoop-dogg-quotes/.

McVey, Eli. 2017. "Chart: Percentage of Cannabis Business Owners and Founders by Race." *Marijuana Business Daily.* Accessed November 23, 2020. https://mjbiz-daily.com/chart-19-cannabis-businesses-owned-founded-racial-minorities/.

———. 2020. "Chart: US Cannabis Industry's Economic Impact Could Hit $130 Billion by 2024." *Marijuana Business Daily.* Accessed July 26, 2021. https://mjbizdaily.com/chart-us-cannabis-industrys-economic-impact-could-hit-130-bil-lion-by-2024/.

McWilliams, John. 1990. *The Protectors: Harry J. Anslinger and the Federal Bureau of Narcotics, 1930–1962.* Newark: University of Delaware Press.

Meadows, Jonah. 2020. "Social Equity Cannabis License Delayed for Scoring Review." *Patch.* Accessed July 16, 2021. https://patch.com/illinois/across-il/so-cial-equity-cannabis-license-lottery-delayed-scoring-review.

Mello, Joseph. 2016a. *The Courts, the Ballot Box, and Gay Rights: How our Governing Institutions Shape the Same-Sex Marriage Debate.* Lawrence: University Press of Kansas.

———. 2016b. "Reluctant Radicals: How Average Citizens Shape Movements for Social Change." *Law and Social Inquiry* 41 (3): 720–41.

———. 2019. "The Right Stuff? Assessing the Use of Rights Discourse in Same-Sex Marriage Ballot Measure Campaigns." *Polity* 51 (4): 724–48.

Meyer, David S. 2004. "Protest and Political Opportunity." *Annual Review of Sociology* 30:125–45.

Meyers, William. 1985. "Crackdown: A Grower Speaks Out." *High Times*, August, 31–36, 71, 97.

Mezey, Naomi. 2003. "Law as Culture." In *Cultural Analysis, Cultural Studies, and the Law*, ed. Austin Sarat and Jonathan Simon, 37–72. Durham, NC: Duke University Press.

Michigan Department of Treasury. 2022. "Adult-Use Marijuana Payments to Be Distributed to Michigan Municipalities, Counties." March 24. Accessed September 5, 2022. https://www.michigan.gov/treasury/about/news/2022/03/24/treasury-adult-use-marijuana-payments-to-be-distributed-to-michigan-municipalities-counties.

Michigan Regulatory Agency. 2021. "Monthly Report: March 1, 2021–March 31, 2021." Accessed September 5, 2022. https://www.michigan.gov/cra/-/media/Project/Websites/cra/Agency-Reports/Statistical-Reports/monthly-report/March_2021_Monthly_Report.pdf.

Miller, Char. 2018. *Where There's Smoke: The Environmental Science, Public Policy, and Politics of Marijuana*. Lawrence: University Press of Kansas.

Minority Cannabis Business Association. 2022. "MCBA National Cannabis Equity Report." file:///C:/Users/jmell/Downloads/MCBA-Arcview-Equity-report.pdf.

Mishler, Elliot. 1986. *Research Interviewing: Context and Narrative*. Cambridge, MA: Harvard University Press.

Morrison, Leslie. 1976. "Interview: A Smuggling Ace." *High Times*, November, 25–32, 40, 112–16.

Mudge, Stephanie. 2008. "What Is Neo-Liberalism?" *Socio-Economic Review* 6 (4): 703–31.

Murray, Charles Shaar. 1989. *Crosstown Traffic: Jimi Hendrix and the Post-War Rock 'n' Roll Revolution*. New York: St. Martin's Press.

Murray, Mellissa. 2012. "What's So New about the New Illegitimacy?" *American University Journal of Gender, Social Policy, and the Law* 20 (3): 387–436.

Murrieta, Ed. 2017. "High Times Magazine Sells to Bob Marley's Son, Others." *San Francisco Chronicle*, June 1. Accessed August 21, 2017. http://www.sfchronicle.com/business/article/High-Times-magazine-sells-to-Bob-Marley-s-son-11186596.php.

National Conference of State Legislatures. 2023. "State Medical Cannabis Laws." Accessed November 17, 2023. https://www.ncsl.org/health/state-medical-cannabis-laws.

New Frontier Data. 2020. "Growth of the U.S. Legal Cannabis Industry." Accessed January 10, 2021. https://newfrontierdata.com/cannabis-insights/growth-of-the-u-s-legal-cannabis-industry/.

Ogden, David. 2009. "Memorandum for Selected United State Attorneys on Investigations and Prosecutions in States Authorizing the Medical Use of Marijuana." Accessed May 27, 2020. https://www.justice.gov/archives/opa/blog/memorandum-selected-united-state-attorneys-investigations-and-prosecutions-states.

Oliver, Pamela E., and Hank Johnston. 2000. "What a Good Idea! Ideologies and Frames in Social Movement Research." *Mobilization* 4 (1): 37–54.

Orenstein, Daniel G. 2020. "Preventing Industry Abuse of Cannabis Equity Programs." *Southern Illinois University Law Journal*. 45: 69–108.

Orenstein, Daniel G., and Stanton A. Glantz. 2020. "The Grassroots of Grass: Cannabis Legalization Ballot Initiative Campaign Contributions and Outcomes, 2004, 2016." *Journal of Health Politics, and Policy, and Law* 45 (1): 73–109.

Pager, Devah. 2007. *Marked: Race, Crime, and Finding Work in an Era of Mass Incarceration.* Chicago: University of Chicago Press.

Papke, David. 1996. "Myth and Meaning: Francis Ford Coppola and Popular Response to the Godfather Trilogy." In *Legal Reelism: Movies as Legal Texts*, ed. John Denvir, 1–22. Urbana-Champaign: University of Illinois Press.

Peake, Gage. 2020. "Launch of Bob Marley Cannabis in WA Heralds Continued Rise of Celeb Cannabis Brands." *Leafly.* Accessed August 8, 2023. https://www.leafly.com/news/industry/launch-bob-marley-cannabis-wa-heralds-continued-rise-celeb-cannabis-brands.

Pisanti, Simona, and Maurizio Bifulco. 2019. "Medical Cannabis: A Plurimillenial History of an Evergreen." *Journal of Cellular Physiology* 234 (6): 8342–51.

Polson, Michael. 2022. "Legalization and Prohibition: Breaks, Continuities, and the Shifting Terms of Racial-Capitalist Governance." In *The Routledge Handbook of Post-Prohibition Cannabis Studies*, ed. Dominic Corva and Joshua Meisel, 36–43. New York: Routledge.

Prescott, J. J., and Sonja Starr. 2020. "Expungement of Criminal Convictions: An Empirical Study." *Harvard Law Review* 133 (8): 2460–2555.

Quinton, Sophie. 2021. "Black-Owned Pot Businesses Remain Rare Despite Diversity Efforts." *PEW*, January 15. Accessed September 4, 2022. https://www.pewtrusts.org/en/research-and-analysis/blogs/stateline/2021/01/15/black-owned-pot-businesses-remain-rare-despite-diversity-efforts.

Rabinow, Paul, and William Sullivan. 1988. *Interpretive Social Science: A Second Look.* Berkeley: University of California Press.

Rapping, Elayne. 2003. *Law and Justice as Seen on TV.* New York: NYU Press.

Rees, Emma. 2018. "Clothes Do Not Make the Woman: What Female Academics Wear Is Subject to Constant Scrutiny." *Times Higher Education*, April 15. Accessed August 12, 2020. https://www.timeshighereducation.com/features/clothes-do-not-make-woman-what-female-academics-wear-subject-constant-scrutiny.

Reiman, Amanda. 2022. "The Intersection of Cannabis Reform and Other Progressive Movements: Opportunities for Interdisciplinary Researchers." In *The Routledge Handbook of Post-Prohibition Cannabis Studies*, ed. Dominic Corva and Joshua Meisel, 336–46. New York: Routledge.

Reinarman, Craig, and Harry Levine. 1997. "Crack in Context: America's Latest Demon Drug." In *Crack in America: Demon Drugs and Social Justice*, ed. Craig Reinarman and Harry Levine, 1–17. Berkeley: University of California Press.

Rios, Carmen. 2015. "You Call It Professionalism; I Call it Professionalism in a Three-Piece Suit." *Everyday Feminism*, February 15. Accessed August 12, 2020. https://everydayfeminism.com/2015/02/professionalism-and-oppression/.

Robinson, Melia. 2016. "How a Silicon Valley Billionaire Helped Get Marijuana

Fully Legalized in California." *Business Insider*, November 9. Accessed October 6, 2020. https://www.businessinsider.com/sean-parker-legalize-marijuana-california-2016-11.

Rodriguez, Agustin, Christina Sava, and Michael Jordan. 2022. "Residency Rules in Cannabis Industry May Not Withstand Constitutional Scrutiny." *Cannabis Law Journal*. Accessed September 27, 2022. https://journal.cannabislawreport.com/troutman-pepper-residency-rules-in-cannabis-industry-may-not-withstand-constitutional-scrutiny/.

Rolling Stone. 2020. "The 500 Greatest Albums of all Time." *Rolling Stone*, September 22. Accessed August 2, 2023. https://www.rollingstone.com/music/music-lists/best-albums-of-all-time-1062063/outkast-aquemini-4-1063184/.

Rosenberg, Gerald L. 1991. *The Hollow Hope: Can Courts Bring about Social Change?* Chicago: University of Chicago Press.

Rossinow, Doug. 1998. *The Politics of Authenticity: Liberalism, Christianity, and the New Left in America*. New York: Columbia University Press.

Sarat, Austin. 2000. "Imagining the Loss of the Father: Loss, Dread, and Mourning in *The Sweet Hereafter*." *Law and Society Review* 34 (1): 3–46.

Schattschneider, E. E. 1960. *The Semisovereign People: A Realist's View of Democracy in America*. New York: Holt, Rinehart, and Winston.

Scheingold, Stuart A. 1974. *The Politics of Rights: Lawyers, Public Policy, and Political Change*. Ann Arbor: University of Michigan Press.

Schlosser, Eric. 2003. *Reefer Madness: Sex, Drugs, and Cheap Labor in the American Black Market*. New York: Houghton Mifflin.

Schlussel, David. 2017. "The Mellow Pot-Smoker: White Individualism in Cannabis Legalization Campaigns." *California Law Review* 105:885–928.

Schmidt, Christopher. 2018. *The Sit-Ins: Protest and Legal Change in the Civil Rights Era*. Chicago: University of Chicago Press.

Schreckinger, Ben. 2020. "How Legal Weed Destroyed a Counterculture Icon." *Politico*, September 4. Accessed January 14, 2021. https://www.politico.com/news/magazine/2020/09/04/high-times-hard-times-404419.

Schroyer, John. 2022. "New York Spending $200 Million on Marijuana Social Equity Properties." *Marijuana Business Daily*, June 21. Accessed September 19, 2022. https://mjbizdaily.com/new-york-spending-200-million-on-marijuana-social-equity-properties/.

Schuba, Tom. 2020. "'Epic Failure' of Illinois' Legal Weed Backers in Springfield to Keep Promise on Diversity." *Chicago Sun-Times*, December 11. Accessed July 16, 2021. https://chicago.suntimes.com/2020/12/11/22166603/marijuana-legalization-recreational-illinois-diversity-innovative-industrial-properties-legal-weed.

———. 2021a. "Infighting Erupts as Minority Pot Shop Applicants Draft Legislation to Resolve the State's Troubled Cannabis Licensing Rollout." *Chicago Sun-Times*, February 23. Accessed July 16, 2021. https://chicago.suntimes.com/cannabis/2021/2/23/22297586/infighting-erupts-minority-pot-shop-applicants-draft-legislation-resolve-troubled-cannabis-rollout.

————. 2021b. "Billions in Black-Market Weed Still Selling in Illinois 18 Months After Marijuana Legalized." *Chicago Sun-Times*, June 14. Accessed July 16, 2021. https://chicago.suntimes.com/cannabis/2021/6/14/22534079/illinois-dispensa-ries-illegal-legal-marijuana-cannabis-pot-bud-sale.

Sentencing Project. 2023. "Growth in Mass Incarceration." Accessed August 7, 2023. https://www.sentencingproject.org/research/.

Seven Hounds Ventures. 2020. "Privateer Holdings." Accessed August 8, 2023. https://7hventures.co/investments-details/privateer-holdings.

Shafer, Raymond P., et al. 1972. "Marihuana: A Signal of Misunderstanding." *Official Report of the National Commission of Marihuana and Drug Abuse*. Accessed June 9, 2020. http://www.druglibrary.org/schaffer/Library/studies/nc/ncmenu.htm.

Silbey, Susan. 2005. "After Legal Consciousness." *Annual Review of Law and Social Science* 1:323–68.

Silvaggio, Anthony. 2018. "Cannabis Agriculture in California: The Environmental Consequences of Prohibition." In *Where There's Smoke: The Environmental Science, Public Policy, and Politics of Marijuana*, ed. Char Miller, 13–28. Lawrence: University Press of Kansas.

Skye, Dan. 2008. "The Happy Warrior: Marc Emery." *High Times*, December, 72.

————. 2011. "Seed Fortunes." *High Times*, August, 54–56.

Smith, Katherine, Frances Stillman, Lee Bone, Norman Yancey, Emmanuel Price, Precilla Belin, and Elizabeth Kromm. 2007. "Buying and Selling 'Loosies' in Baltimore: The Informal Exchange of Cigarettes in the Community Context." *Journal of Urban Health* 84 (4): 494–507.

Solomon, Robert. 2020. "Racism and Its Effects on Cannabis Research." *Cannabis and Cannabinoid Research* 5 (1): 2–5.

Spencer, Katherine B., Amanda K. Charbonneau, and Jack Glaser. 2016. "Implicit Bias and Policing." *Social & Personal Psychology Compass* 10 (1): 50–63.

Starr, Paul. 2017. *The Social Transformation of American Medicine: The Rise of a Sovereign Profession and the Making of a Vast Industry*. 2nd ed. New York: Basic Books.

Stephens, Michelle A. 1998. "Babylon's 'Natural Mystic': The North American Music Industry, the Legend of Bob Marley, and the Incorporation of Trans Nationalism." *Cultural Studies* 12 (2): 139–67.

Stroup, Keith. 2013. *Its NORML to Smoke Pot: The 40 Year Fight for Cannabis Smokers' Rights*. New York: High Times/Trans High Corp.

Tarrow, Sidney G. 2011. *Power in Movement: Social Movements and Contentious Politics*. 3rd ed. Cambridge: Cambridge University Press.

Thompson, Hunter S. 1970. "Freak Power in the Rockies." *Rolling Stone* 67 (October 1). Rpt. in *The Great Shark Hunt: Strange Tales from a Strange Time* (New York: Simon and Schuster, 1973), 151–75.

————. 1971. *Fear and Loathing in Las Vegas: A Savage Journey to the Heart of the American Dream*. New York: Random House.

Tyler, Tom. 1990. *Why People Obey the Law*. New Haven, CT: Yale University Press.

Uitti, Jacob. 2022. "Behind the Meaning of 'I Shot the Sheriff' by Bob Marley." *American Songwriter*. Accessed August 2, 2023. https://americansongwriter.com/behind-the-meaning-of-the-song-i-shot-the-sheriff-by-bob-marley/.

Wacquant, Loïc. 2009. *Punishing the Poor: The Neoliberal Government of Social Insecurity*. Durham, NC: Duke University Press.

Walsh, Mathew. 2020. "The State of the Marijuana Black Market." *Brown Political Review*, January. Accessed July 16, 2021. https://brownpoliticalreview.org/2020/01/the-state-of-the-marijuana-black-market/.

Walter, Shoshana. 2016. "In Secretive Marijuana Industry, Whispers of Abuse and Trafficking." *Reveal*. Accessed July 30, 2021. https://revealnews.org/article/in-secretive-marijuana-industry-whispers-of-abuse-and-trafficking/.

Warf, Barney. 2014. "High Points: An Historical Geography of Cannabis." *Geographical Review* 104 (4): 414–48.

Weisheit, Ralph A. 1992. *Domestic Marijuana: A Neglected Industry*. New York: Greenwood Press.

West, Steven L., and Keri K. O'Neal. 2004. "Project D.A.R.E. Outcome Effectiveness Revisited." *American Journal of Public Health* 94 (6): 1027–29.

White, Timothy. 2006. *Catch a Fire: The Life of Bob Marley*. Revised ed. New York: Holt.

Whitney, Beau. 2022. "U.S. Cannabis Business Conditions Survey Report Reveals Critical Concerns for the Cannabis Industry in 2022." *National Cannabis Industry Association*. Accessed September 14, 2022. https://thecannabisindustry.org/u-s-cannabis-business-conditions-survey-report-reveals-critical-concerns-for-the-cannabis-industry-in-2022/.

Williams, Patricia. 1991. *The Alchemy of Race and Rights*. Cambridge, MA: Harvard University Press.

Williamson, Elizabeth. 2019. "Once and Enemy, Now a Promoter of Legalized Pot." *New York Times*, June 4, A1.

Yanow, Dvora. 2006. "Neither Rigorous nor Objective? Interrogating Criteria for Knowledge Claims in Interpretive Science." In *Interpretation and Method: Empirical Research Methods and the Interpretive Turn*, ed. Dvora Yanow and Peregrine Schwartz-Shea, 67–87. London: M. E. Sharpe.

Young, Simon. 2023. "Here Are the 20 Longest-Charting Albums in the History of the Billboard 200." *Louder*. Accessed August 2, 2023. https://www.loudersound.com/news/here-are-the-20-longest-charting-albums-in-the-history-of-the-billboard-200.

Zemans, Frances Kahn. 1983. "Legal Mobilization: The Neglected Role of the Law in the Political System." *American Political Science Review* 77:690–703.

Zong, Jie, and Jeanne Batalova. 2014. "Mexican Immigrants in the United States." *Migration Policy Institute*. Accessed August 12, 2022. https://www.migrationpolicy.org/article/mexican-immigrants-united-states-2013.

Cases Cited

Brown v. Board of Education of Topeka. 1954. 347 U.S. 483.
Gonzales v. Raich. 2005. 545 U.S. 1.
McCulloch v. Maryland. 1819. 17 U.S. 316.
United States v. Randall. 1976. 104 Wash. D.L. Rep. 2249-2252.

Index

activism: maintaining motivation for, 133–36, 145; sense of purpose derived from, 135–36. *See also* cannabis reform activists

Adult Use of Marijuana Act (AUMA), 67

African Americans: culture, embrace by white counterculture of 1960s, 26–27, 139, 145, 146–48; factors complicating legal cannabis use, 77–78; higher rate of arrests for cannabis, 77; learned avoidance of interactions with authorities, 36; learned avoidance of politics, and cannabis reform, 36–37; male, as routinely shot by police, 35; police harassment of, 77; psychic damage from over-policing, 35–37; reluctance to engage with cannabis industry, 36. *See also* communities of color; minority access to dispensary licenses

Alinsky, Saul, 63, 133, 136

Amorphia, 28

Anslinger, Harry, 25

Armstrong, Louis, 146

arrests for cannabis: current number per year, 8; decline with legalization,
8, 79, 160n5; in states with cannabis legalization, 143; targeting of communities of color, 8–9, 80–81, 144, 159–60n4

AUMA. *See* Adult Use of Marijuana Act

"back to the landers," as early growers of cannabis, 28–30, 32

ballot measures on medical cannabis: in California, 46–47; legal gray area created by, 47–49; states passing, 47

Beatles, 148

Berry, Chuck, 148

Black Power movement, 147

Black Reconstruction in America (Du Bois), 11

Bob Marley and the Wailers: alarm caused by, in US, 1–2, 151; *Burnin'*, 1–2, 139, 150–51, 154; *To Catch a Fire*, 150; *Exodus*, 152, 154; *Kaya*, 152, 154; *Legend*, 139, 153–55; radical politics of music, 150–51, 152–53; *Survival*, 152–53; violence surrounding, 149. *See also* Marley, Robert Nesta "Bob"

Boehner, John, 56, 161n2

Boston Freedom Rally, 119

THE CULTURAL LIVES OF LAW
Austin Sarat, Editor

The Cultural Lives of Law series brings insights and approaches from cultural studies to law and tries to secure for law a place in cultural analysis. Books in the series focus on the production, interpretation, consumption, and circulation of legal meanings. They take up the challenges posed as boundaries collapse between as well as within cultures, and as the circulation of legal meanings becomes more fluid. They also attend to the ways law's power in cultural production is renewed and resisted.

Chloé Deambrogio, *Judging Insanity, Punishing Difference: A History of Mental Illness in the Criminal Court*
2024

Daniel LaChance and Paul Kaplan, *Crimesploitation: Crime, Punishment, and Pleasure on Reality Television*
2022

Nesam McMillan, *Imagining the International: Crime, Justice, and the Promise of Community*
2020

Jeffrey R. Dudas, *Raised Right: Fatherhood in Modern American Conservatism*
2017

Renée Ann Cramer, *Pregnant with the Stars: Watching and Wanting the Celebrity Baby Bump*
2015

Sora Y. Han, *Letters of the Law: Race and the Fantasy of Colorblindness*
2015

Marianne Constable, *Our Word Is Our Bond: How Legal Speech Acts*
2014

Joshua C. Wilson, *The Street Politics of Abortion: Speech, Violence, and America's Culture Wars*
2013

Irus Braverman, *Zooland: The Institution of Captivity*
2012

Nora Gilbert, *Better Left Unsaid: Victorian Novels, Hays Code Films, and the Benefits of Censorship*
2012

Edited by Winnifred Fallers Sullivan, Robert A. Yelle, and Mateo Taussig-Rubbo, *After Secular Law*
2011

Keith J. Bybee, *All Judges Are Political—Except When They Are Not: Acceptable Hypocrisies and the Rule of Law*
2010

Susan Sage Heinzelman, *Riding the Black Ram: Law, Literature, and Gender*
2010

David M. Engel and Jaruwan S. Engel, *Tort, Custom, and Karma: Globalization and Legal Consciousness in Thailand*
2010

Ruth A. Miller, *Law in Crisis: The Ecstatic Subject of Natural Disaster*
2009

Ravit Reichman, *The Affective Life of Law: Legal Modernism and the Literary Imagination*
2009

Edited by David M. Engel and Michael McCann, *Fault Lines: Tort Law as Cultural Practice*
2008

William P. MacNeil, *Lex Populi: The Jurisprudence of Popular Culture*
2007

Edited by Austin Sarat and Christian Boulanger, *The Cultural Lives of Capital Punishment: Comparative Perspectives*
2005

Printed in the USA
CPSIA information can be obtained
at www.ICGtesting.com
JSHW020509270424
61957JS00004B/4